*. . . Finding Answers to
Why Good People Die
Tragic and Early Deaths*

WHAT OTHERS ARE SAYING
About This book

Pastor Adelaja's passion for life and death shines through in this tribute to Dr. Myles Munroe. Here he looks death in the face and gives the church hope. He takes the one subject that is so misunderstood by this modern narcissistic generation and opens the door to truly comprehending what lies beyond for the faithful. If that were all he did this book would be wonderful. Pastor Adelaja, however, goes to the next level and shows us how to live with the understanding that Dr. Munroe so clearly lived by, the understanding that we are each called to fulfil our purpose in this life and "die empty." Herein lies the freedom to truly live a life worthy of our Lord and Savior. Thank you, Pastor Adelaja for working through the pain to show us a better way--the way! Like Dr. Munroe, let's all fulfil our destiny and leave the graveyards of the world empty of everything but the dust of these shells we temporarily call home!

Joel Thornton
President and General Counsel
International Human Rights Group

Sunday Adelaja's book, "MYLES MUNROE . . . Finding Answers to why Good People die tragic and early deaths" is a masterpiece! I question whether there has ever been a book written like it before. It is not only a sobering understanding, of how we as believers should view death. It is a heartfelt tribute and thorough analysis of a true Kingdom General of our generation - Dr. Myles Munroe.

Other than Jesus, Sunday Adelaja may be the first to ever "answer" the question of life and death so accurately, thoroughly, and biblically. This book dares to uncover the glorious truth regarding the mystery of death, and at the same time makes you want to jump up and make the very most of your day!

The questions surrounding the premature or tragic death of believers are finally answered. Sunday Adelaja has done it again, courageously explaining one of life's greatest mysteries.

Derek Schneider
President of History Makers Academy
Founder of History Makers Society

Thank you Apostle Sunday for writing this book, it will go a long way to impact lives and bring meaning to the subject of death and what it means in the life of a believer. I believe leaders and people who stand for progress will benefit from reading this book.

Kindly permit me to say that I'm endorsing this book because it is a timely one, and also it is a tribute to my friend Dr. Myles Munroe who was a man with passion and enthusiasm for the Kingdom of God; a champion of the principles of the Kingdom of God in the Earth who advanced the Kingdom message outside the church walls. A true Diplomat, a General in our era, a Wise Master Builder, a Standard Raiser and a Great Leader.

In 1990, I invited Dr. Monroe to St. Martin to impart the leaders of the Nation, Church, Businesses, Government, etc. He shared a song with the following words "I don't know how long

I'll be here. For Jesus said He'll come again; And I know I'm going with Him when He calls my name. Oh Oh Oh, I wanna be ready, Oh, Oh, I wanna be ready". Today the words of this song and the transition of Dr. Munroe is a call for us to be ready.

In this book, Apostle Sunday has made justice to the question of death, tragedy and happenings that we cannot always have a clue about. It's about living a legacy in the earth. Let us arise and do what God is asking us to do without reservation.

Thank you Pastor Sunday for this work and letting the world have vital answers and continue to appreciate Dr. Munoe's Legacy.

Apostle Hilton Albert.
St. Martin French West Indies.

I would like to encourage everyone in the body Christ to read this book! We have all asked the question, "Why do good people die seemingly before their time?" After the death of Dr. Munroe, the church is asking . . . how could the man who gave the church a deeper understanding of purpose, die so tragically?

Pastor Sunday uses great spiritual insight as well as tremendous biblical knowledge to answer these questions. This book is a must read!

Bishop Michael Badger
Bethesda World Harvest International Church

This book that Pastor Sunday has written goes a long way in helping to answer the question why the passing of Dr. Myles & Ruth Munroe and those who also transitioned in that tragic plane accident. It was through Dr. Myles Munroe that God confirmed the message of the Kingdom to me, and its through this book that Pastor Sunday is echoing much of what Dr. Munroe wanted people to understand about death.

This book will help you to come to know and understand that it is not about how you die that is important. The question will be how did you live? What was your contribution to society? What good did you leave? Dr. Myles Munroe travelled the globe preaching and teaching Purpose, and The Kingdom of God, Leadership Principles, and the importance of passing on what God has given to you, so that your legacy; what you've created will outlive you and help others to live successfully. Pastor Sunday has captured both the motivation and heart of Dr. Munroe and his ministry and the heart of the Father towards us in the passing of His great Ambassador.

Thank you Pastor Sunday, for having the sensitivity of heart towards the Holy Spirit in being open to the revelation of the certainty of death, and its impossibility to kill a vision or visionary who has come from God. You've helped us to understand all the more that it is not in how one dies but how they lived that matters most. Thank you Pastor Sunday for being a voice and not an echo of religious men's ideas. This book is much needed in bringing clarity of God's wisdom in this hour.

Dr. Leonard Robinson
Sr. Pastor
Kingdom Vision Ministries International,
Philadelphia, PA

MYLES MUNROE

... FINDING ANSWERS TO WHY GOOD PEOPLE DIE TRAGIC AND EARLY DEATHS

SUNDAY ADELAJA

MYLES MUNROE ... FINDING ANSWERS TO WHY GOOD PEOPLE DIE TRAGIC AND EARLY DEATHS
By Sunday Adelaja

Published by
Cornerstone Publishing
New York
Phone: +1(516)-547-4999
info@thecornerstonepublishers.com
www.thecornerstonepublishers.com
In partnership With
GOLDEN PEN PUBLISHING LTD, UK

This book or parts thereof may not be reproduced in any form, stored in a retrieval system or transmitted in any form by any means—electronic, mechanical, photocopy, recording or otherwise—without prior written permission of the publisher, except as provided by United States of America copyright law.

Unless otherwise noted, Bible quotations are taken from the Holy Bible, New King James Version. Copyright 1982 by Thomas Nelson, Inc., publishers. Used by permission.

Scripture quotations marked KJV are from the King James Version of the Bible.

Scripture quotations marked NIV are from the Holy Bible, New International version. Copyright © 1973, 1978, 1984, International Bible Society. Used by permission.

Scripture quotations marked AMP are from the Holy Bible, Amplified Version. Copyright © 1954, 1958, 1962, 1964, 1965, Zondervan Publishing House. Used by permission.

Cover design by: Cornerstone Concept and Design
Copyright © 2015 by **Sunday Adelaja**
ALL RIGHTS RESERVED
International Standard Book Number: 978-1-908040-56-5
Printed in the United States of America

DISCLAIMER

*The ideas, information and theological teachings contained in this book are from the **AUTHOR'S PERSPECTIVE** on the subject matter. This book is written independent of family and ministries of Late Dr Myles Munroe.*

DEDICATION

To all those people who had one time or the other lost their loved and dear ones, starting from the family and church of my dear friend and brother **Dr Myles Munroe.**

Part of the proceeds from the sale of this book will be going to support Myles Munroe Ministries Worldwide.

CONTENTS

FOREWORD   **19**

PREFACE   **21**

INTRODUCTION   **25**

CHAPTER 1 27
SO, WHY SUCH A TRAGIC DEATH?

- Preciousness of Saints' Death
- What If the Death Was Violent?
- Supremacy of God
- Is Ceremonial Blessing Compulsory?

CHAPTER 2 33
THE FREEDOM OF DEATH

- The Elders' Perspective
- The "Underage" Question
- Death's Defeat
- Beautiful "Tragedy"

CHAPTER 3..49
STILL, WHY DIE SO YOUNG?
- Understanding Biblical Promises of Long Life

CHAPTER 4..67
WHEN DEATH IS GAIN
- Perception of Death in the Old and New Testaments
- Christ's Perception of Death
- Our Victory over Death
- Are We Strangers or Settlers?

CHAPTER 5..81
FROM EARLY DEATH TO TIMELESS FAME
- Detailed Examples
- Munroe's Experience

CHAPTER 6..89
DYING EMPTY: A MORE NOBLE CONCERN
- What Does it Mean to Die Empty?
- Scriptural Examples
- Contemporary Examples
- A Word of Caution
- Dr Munroe's View on Dying Empty
- Additional Excerpt

CHAPTER 7..105
WHERE ARE YOUR TREASURES - HEAVEN OR EARTH?

- A Question to Answer
- Danger of Being Worldly-Minded

CHAPTER 8..119
MYLES MUNROE: THE MAN AND HIS MINISTRY

- The Making of a Champion
- Birth of His Ministry
- Testimonies and Tributes
- His Impact in Death

CHAPTER 9..135
LIFE LESSONS FROM DR MYLES MUNROE

- Emergence from the Shadows
- A Real and Genuine Life
- Marriage and Family Life
- A Teacher with Distinction
- A Loving Personal Touch
- A Global Mentor

CHAPTER 10..157

THE LEGACIES OF DR. MUNROE'S LIFE

- His Church – The Bahamas Faith Ministries International (BFMI)
- His Leadership Organisations
- His Contributions To The Bahamas

CHAPTER 11..165

DR. MUNROE'S REVELATIONS TO THE WORLD

- Munroe on God's Kingdom
- Munroe on Leadership
- Munroe on Turning Followers into Leaders
- Munroe on Purpose
- Munroe on Third World Nations
- Munroe on Marriage
- Munroe on Family Values
- Last Word

ABOUT PASTOR SUNDAY ADELAJA................195

FOREWORD

I want to first of all commend Pastor Sunday Adelaja for taking the time to put this work together. Once again, you have blazed the trail, and the rest will be history making and life changing experience for millions.

It is a privilege for me to write the foreword for such a timely, informative, educative and life-changing treasure, as I'll like to refer to this book. In 1984 when I first met Dr. Myles Munroe, I was awakened to the fact that everything in life has a purpose and when the purpose is not known, abuse is inevitable. With his transition, millions of people are asking why this way and why so soon? Finally, the answer to the question is here.

I strongly believe this book will help you find purpose and appreciate what you could ignorantly abuse. Reading the pages of this book, I kept asking myself if I've ever come across a book similar to this, and my answer is an emphatic NO!

This is not a book about tragedy and death as much as it is a book about understanding life and fulfillment. Beyond a tribute, the book seeks to get rid of misconceptions about death and transitioning which unfortunately, many believers dread to think about.

In the eleventh chapter of this book, not only has Pastor Sunday laid out a legacy and insight into a world of Dr. Myles Munroe that many wouldn't have had access to if this book was not written, but he has doubtlessly answered questions that have languished in the minds of people for centuries.

It was Dr. Myles who said, "Life is not measured by its duration, but by its contribution." This is why you have access to this treasure of understanding death from a Kingdom perspective that will align your life and make you kingdom minded as the champion in you emerges.

As we remember Dr. Myles Munroe who has gone ahead and left empty, I wish to remind you in his words that by reading this book you will know "You weren't born just to live a life and to die, you were born to accomplish something specifically," and that "The greatest tragedy in life is not death, but a life without a purpose."

Finally, I wish to say that those who lead today and those who aspire to leadership tomorrow have a great deal to learn from this book whether they seek to serve Kingdom Community, business or government. The mystery is unveiled. Go for the gold!

Dr. Albert S. L. Kitcher
World Transformation Church (Founder)
KAIROS Group Initiatives (CEO)

PREFACE

On Monday, 10th November 2014, I, like most people, woke up to the shocking news that Dr Myles Munroe and his beloved wife, Ruth, had died alongside seven others in a tragic plane crash the previous night. I was heartbroken, and understandably so. Dr Myles and his wife had impacted my life, ministry and our whole Russian speaking world in a spectacular way.

Dr Myles was not just a pastor, teacher and minister of the gospel – he was, first of all, a man, a full-blooded human being. He was a man who genuinely worked hard to transform himself to reflect the image and likeness of God.

Myles Munroe made you feel you were his peer. He did everything to make you feel at home. I recall the first time I met him in 1999. He and Ruth had decided to attend one of our conferences here at the Embassy of God, Kiev, Ukraine, for the very first time. However, a few days to their arrival, I was taken ill with chickenpox. Of course, with that kind of infection, I needed to be isolated. But when Dr Myles arrived, he insisted on seeing me. When he came into the room, I asked him to stay away from me so he would not get infected. To my surprise, however, he came right at me, hugging me. What he said was even more amazing:

"…Rub those wounds on my skin. Rub your body

against my body because we are brothers; we are covenant brothers, we are brother's keepers. Let your problem become my problem, let your challenge become my challenge, let's share this chickenpox together, let's carry the burden together…"

I was stunned. I was stirred. And from that day, Myles Munroe won my heart. He quickly became one of my closest friends, and much more – he was a partner, an elder brother, a confidant.

A day later, when the conference began, I made another discovery about this extraordinary personality. I discovered that Myles Munroe was a teacher, in every sense of the word. At first, I was baffled. I had never heard him speak and I was sure he had never heard me either; yet he spoke as I would have spoken. I had never heard anybody preach the same kind of message that I preached. So, to hear Dr Myles Munroe do it with such brilliance and eloquence totally captivated me. Most preachers would understand me when I say that there comes a point in your ministry when you find it difficult knowing whom to listen to. But from that week till date, Myles Munroe became one of the few people in the world whom I can readily listen to and learn valuable lessons.

Myles Munroe shook my world. After his messages, testimonies and exhortations in our church, I vowed to discover God for myself in a new way. He had sparked a new hunger in me that drove me to God and self-education like never before. Through this, my ministry took on a totally different dimension. We started to have social, economic and political influence, just as he taught us. Members of our church began to discover and pursue their life purposes, and thus began an explosive and all-round transformation in my ministry!

Let me share another secret with you about the humanity of

PREFACE

this great giant of God. Each time I met Dr Myles, he would run towards me, with his arms wide open, as in a warm embrace, then he would fall on his knees, with his head bowed down. This was one of the biggest acts of humility you would ever see, especially coming from such a renowned personality like Dr Myles Munroe.

Dr Myles spent so much to keep coming to Ukraine to help us build a world-class church. He was embarrassed many times by immigration officers at the point of entry; yet, brotherly love prevailed on him to overlook all the challenges that it took to partner with a brother and help a friend.

When the attacks on me and our church from the Ukrainian government became very fierce, with all forms of false allegations, court cases and threats, Dr Myles continued to keep in touch, despite his busy schedule, to assure us of his prayers. Even though I could not travel out of Ukraine at a time, Dr Myles was always sending messages to ascertain my well-being and that of the church.

The last I heard of Myles Munroe was when he sent a message through a mutual friend who was visiting Ukraine from Israel, where Dr Myles had been speaking. He wanted me to know he was coming to see me soon. He said, "Tell Pastor Sunday, he is the most strategic person I have ever met, I will be with him there soon."

Sadly, that was never to happen. I was no longer to be privileged to receive the embrace of my brother on this side of eternity.

> Beloved Dr Myles, it's clear to me that you are no longer the one to be with me soon; I am the one to be with you – in our heavenly Father's home. Rest in peace, my friend. Rest in peace, my brother. Rest in peace, my confidant. Rest in peace, my inspiration.

Rest in peace, God's General. Rest in peace, teacher of men. Rest in peace, man of purpose.

You have lived a full life, poured out to humanity; great shall be your reward. Rest on, Dr Myles Munroe. Adieu, Dr Ruth Munroe - until we all meet again at the bosom of our Lord and Saviour, Jesus Christ.

Pastor Sunday Adelaja
Kiev, Ukraine

INTRODUCTION

I was moved to write this book because, first of all, it is the first anniversary of Dr Myles Munroe's death. I therefore considered it timely to do so. Secondly, following the release of a video with the same title on social media, many friends and followers of our ministry requested for a related publication. There were also some who could not download the video due to the challenge of Internet accessibility. This gives them the opportunity to get the message in textual form.

I also think it is proper to improve on the article that accompanied the video by establishing some of the points scripturally. From the comments I received on my social media pages, I understand that many Christians do not seem to see the Biblical perspective of my submissions. I therefore wish to encourage everyone to get a better understanding of that article by reading this book. Even if you have watched the video, I believe you will find this book more illuminating, as some of the fundamental principles not mentioned in the video are reviewed here.

I am a covenant brother to Dr Myles Munroe; therefore I am compelled to respond to the numerous insinuations that have been made regarding the circumstances of his home-going. As covenant people, we know that the conditions and terms of a covenant require that one party stands for the other if the need arises. I therefore wish to give a comprehensive explanation to what I think God is trying to tell us through the death of Dr Myles and his entourage.

I equally believe that this book will go a long way to support and encourage people everywhere, who have lost or will lose their loved ones either by tragic or controversial circumstances. One of the questions that surface on a daily basis in the minds of Christians worldwide is: how is it possible that brothers and sisters who had served God all their lives can suffer and die in controversial or even tragic circumstances? Since after Dr Munroe's departure, I have heard comments from people. Generally, whether it is sincere Christians or scoffing cynics, the questions remain the same:

- How is it possible that Dr Myles could die such a tragic death?
- How could a man that had given his life to serve the Lord, die in such a way?
- How can it be that Christians who serve God faithfully, who are not living an ungodly lifestyle, can lose their lives in such a tragic way like a plane crash?

Actually, if these questions only came from cynics and critics, I might not have bothered to respond. However, I must admit that even members of my own church and so many other sincere Christians were having the same confusion. So, this is my way of doing something about it.

I feel obligated to answer a few of the emerging questions because, as already noted, I am a covenant brother to Dr Myles Munroe. According to the conditions of this covenant, I am compelled to respond. The terms of our covenant compel me to answer where a brother can no longer speak for himself.

Chapter 1

SO, WHY SUCH A TRAGIC DEATH?

Let me begin the answer to this vital question by quickly looking at the concept of death itself. The medical dictionary describes death as "the cessation of all vital functions of the body including the heartbeat, brain activity (including the brain stem), and breathing." The Stanford Encyclopaedia of Philosophy simply defines it as "life's ending."

However, while there may be some elements of truth in the way scientists and philosophers see death, the simplest and most accurate explanation of death is found in Ecclesiastes 12:7:

> "Then the dust will return to the earth as it was, and the spirit will return to God who gave it"
> **(Ecclesiastes 12:7)**

So, the essence of death, especially for the believer, is to set the spirit man free from the captivity of the body, so it can return to its Maker. And clearly, as the above scripture implies, it really doesn't matter the nature of the incident that releases the spirit from that bondage; what matters is that the spirit returns to its Source as soon as it is summoned.

As the same scripture passage also reveals, the body that is left behind after the spirit is gone is merely a "shell" and it actually returns to the dust, from where it emerged. One key revelation in this biblical description of death is that it is the state of the spirit man in a person that determines who they really are and what they do, and not their physical composition. So, when someone mentions "tragic death" in reference to a believer like Dr Munroe, the description is not true in actual sense. What suffers tragedy is the body, which is actually nothing but a perishable casing for the real being.

The creation story clearly reveals to us that as at the time man was created from the dust, he was practically nothing. He only became something when God breathed (imparted spirit) into him.

> And the Lord God formed man of the dust of the ground, and breathed into his nostrils the breath of life; and man became a living being.
> **(Genesis 2:7)**

What does this show us? That what makes a man alive, active and aspirational is the life of God in him. Consequently, whatever achievements anyone makes on earth, however vibrant, productive, energetic, inspirational, affectionate and indispensable they may seem to us, it is not about their physical prowess but the spirit that lives in them. This means that they don't necessarily belong to the world or even to their families but to the Lord. It is for this reason that the death of a saint is precious in the sight of the Lord – as the spirit swiftly reunites with God who created it in the first place.

Therefore, it doesn't matter so much to God and it doesn't really matter to the person involved "how" death occurs – so long as the spirit is still in tune with God. Who cares about how the shell of an egg is cracked as long as the omelette tastes good? God is not interested in the body as in the soul. That is why Jesus said we should not bother about damage or destruction inflicted on our bodies by persecutors, but to be careful about the state of our souls.

> "And do not fear those who kill the body but cannot kill the soul. But rather fear Him who is able to destroy both soul and body in hell"
> **(Matthew 10:28)**

It is also for the same reason that Paul the Apostle said, "Therefore we do not lose heart. Even though our outward man is perishing, yet the inward man is being renewed day by day" (2 Corinthians 4:16). He said they were not bothered if their bodies perished as long as their inward man remained perpetually renewed and rested in God. Compare this assurance from Paul to the declaration of Stephen, the first martyr. Even as his body was being battered and his bones being broken with stones, only one thing mattered to him – his spirit. "And they stoned Stephen as he was calling on God and saying, Lord Jesus, receive my spirit." (Acts 7:59).

J.R Miller, in his writing, *Stephen the First Martyr* said, "to Stephen, dying was only breathing out his soul into the hands of Jesus Christ! He knew it was not death—but life, which was before him. His body was being mangled and broken—but his spirit, his real self, could not be harmed. Beyond the strange mystery of death—Jesus waits to receive the departing spirit. Death is only a gateway through which the soul passes—and then life and glory burst upon the vision of the emancipated spirit!"

> Indeed, as Christians, it is rather unfitting to be overly concerned about the physical condition in which a person dies. God knows better. Our concern should rather be the state of the soul. A soul that is damaged by sin or unproductive living is in a more tragic and worrisome state.

We must also understand that the main source of conflict and confusion on such matters is often our religious backgrounds and dogmas. God's perspective on death is different from ours.

PRECIOUSNESS OF SAINTS' DEATH

Let me focus a little on this wonderful verse of Scripture that says, "Precious in the sight of the Lord is the death of his saints"(Psalm 116:15).

This really should stir our curiosity and indeed make us rethink our perception of death. If death were to be as horrible as we tend to think, why should God consider the death of His saints precious? Why should He be glad about it? Is He being sadistic? Not at all! The reality is that our perception of death is often wrong. God sees the death of His saints – His beloved children, who mean so much Him - as a PROMOTION for them!

Why would God think this way? It's because death, to the saint of God, is the portal to endless bliss! It is a release from temptations, afflictions, infirmities, conflicts and sorrows.

I want you to note that the verse doesn't say that what makes the death of a saint precious is the way they died or how long they lived, but the fact that they are "saints" and they are coming home. This means that, to God, the death of a saint is ever precious, whether or not the saint is young, middle-aged or aged. In God's eyes, it is still something very precious.

WHAT IF THE DEATH WAS VIOLENT?

Another significant perspective on the tragic death of Christians and God's servants is revealed to us in Isaiah 57:1:

> "The righteous perisheth, and no man layeth it to heart: and merciful men are taken away, none considering that the righteous is taken away from the evil to come."
> **Isaiah 57:1 (KJV)**

Now, look at this: **"The righteous perisheth…"** This might have sounded strange and outrageous to many, if it had not come from God's own word, the Bible. Yes, the righteous can perish, but not in punitive or everlasting terms. To "perish", according to the dictionary, is "to suffer death, typically in a violent, sudden or untimely way." In other words, to perish is to die tragically and untimely. Does this bear any semblance to the death of Dr Munroe and his team in that ghastly crash? Exactly so!

It is obvious then that God makes provision for tragic death, even for the righteous, in the scriptures. The importance that God attaches to scripture references like this is to diffuse confusion about such death and to bring understanding to His people. British clergyman and writer, John Angell James, in his writing, *The Death of Eminent Ministers, a Public Loss* said that, "neither great talents, nor eminent virtues, nor extensive usefulness, can secure for their possessor a longer exemption from the stroke of death—than falls to the lot of humanity in general…There is, indeed, no border country, no neutral territory, no sacred enclosure, within which the holy and benevolent may retire to carry on their labours, and protract their usefulness, secure from the pursuit of disease and death."

The same verse of Scripture says, **"...and no man layeth it to heart..."** This statement denotes confusion and lack of understanding from people. God knows people may not understand why things like this should happen and they will question and query Him on the matter; especially the religious-minded, who will not understand such a tragic death in comparison to the case of Abraham, who lived for so long and died peacefully.

But, then, why would God allow His servant to die in any other way than that of Abraham or Jacob? Could a good God be so inconsistent and unjust to "repay" faithful servants with tragic death? This actually is part of what makes our God a God of unsearchable wisdom, a God of mystery and a God of incomprehensible depth. God cannot be put in a box. God cannot be predicted, and He cannot be fully understood.

> "O the depth of the riches both of the wisdom and knowledge of God! How unsearchable are his judgments, and his ways past finding out!"
> **(Romans 11:33).**

SUPREMACY OF GOD

Again, dear friend, please note that the word perish in Isaiah 57:1 does not refer to worldly people; it refers to the righteous. The God of love, the God of compassion, the God of depth and the God of wisdom gives room for the righteous to perish for reasons only best known to Him. Beyond that, God also would allow good and "...merciful men..." (These are men that are much better than average men) to be taken at a time or in a way that most people would not expect.

Are you confused?

Well, these are the things that make God G-O-D! He is sovereign. He is supreme. And He is surpassing in wisdom, knowledge and understanding!

The majority of the challenges that we encounter in life often stem from wanting to know what God has kept away from us for our good (Deuteronomy 29:29). The human nature in us always wants to be in charge, and that includes reading the mind of God Himself. We see this reflected in Saul, the first king of Israel, when he consulted the witch at Endor to seek a medium on the outcome of the battle between the Israelites and the Philistines. And we know he heard what he was not supposed to hear (1 Samuel 28).

Our insatiable curiosity to always know what God has kept away from us, especially as it relates to the loss of loved ones, exposes our lack of trust in God's judgement. But, in reality, this should not be the way to respond to the departure of these saints of God, particularly when we know they walked with God faithfully and carried out their services sincerely. Our very attitude should be to trust God, even when we don't understand why tragedy happens. He understands what we don't.

Now, this is very important from the verse: **"…none considering that the righteous is taken away from the evil to come."**

> There are several things God sees that no man sees. At any given point in any tragic story and in all unfathomable misfortunes, there is something that God is seeing which you are not seeing. When we only consider our own point of view, we are not always aware of the blind spots in our understanding.

This lack of understanding often leads to confusion, disillusionment and disappointment.

The passage above tells us that we should consider that maybe these men are actually taken away from some form of evil that is to come. This evil could be global or personal. If you could only see behind the scenes as God sees, you might end up rejoicing about what you had earlier called tragic.

IS CEREMONIAL BLESSING COMPULSORY?

One person who was apparently bewildered by the manner of Dr Myles' death made reference to Jacob (in Genesis 49:1) and said, "Jacob, when he was about to die, gathered members of his family, prophesied over them and prayed for them before passing. How could such a great man of God like Myles Munroe, die in such a tragic and sudden way-so different from someone like Jacob?"

Again, I would like to point out that the way you die really doesn't matter in the context of eternity. When someone leaves this physical world, it is really we who are left that are more concerned about how the death occurred.

As regards having a chance to bless your family before passing, Dr Myles did that for over thirty years! He had been prophesying and praying for both his biological and spiritual children and did not need any ceremonial family blessing before he departed.

That was just Dr Myles' lifestyle. He probably blessed as many of his children (spiritual and biological) as he could on that same Sunday, before the tragic incident. He lived that way on a regular basis.

Chapter 2

THE FREEDOM OF DEATH

There is no denying that tragic deaths, especially those resulting from fatal accidents, sometimes involve mangled bodies. However, it is important to note that as soon as a person's spirit leaves their body, they are just as whole as when they were in the flesh, except that they are much younger, more attractive, and perfect. They are now in a "glorified" body.

No matter how good-looking someone is here on earth, no matter how whole they think they are in their physical body, it would hardly compare with their glorified body. Once they cross over to eternity, their earthly body would be as ugly as that of someone who had suffered some kind of tragic death.

As a pastor for over twenty years, I have listened to stories of individuals who had had extraordinary experiences about death and the afterlife. I remember one particular story of a woman who died in her hospital bed. She was a young woman who was quite beautiful and fashionable in her earthly body. However, when her spirit suddenly left her body, she found herself standing on the rooftop, looking down at the doctors and family members surrounding her body.

Puzzled by what she saw, she asked herself, *"What has happened?"* She then began reaching down, trying unsuccessfully to touch her family members. Then she took a closer look at the body on the bed and asked in horror, *"Who is that...?"* When it dawned on her that it was her old body she was seeing, she couldn't believe it. It looked so repulsive!

Scottish theologian and philosopher, Thomas Boston, once said, "Death makes the greatest beauty so loathsome, that it must be buried out of sight!" Puritan preacher and theologian, Thomas Watson also said, "One scarcely knows their friends, they are so disfigured by death! The eyes are hollow, the jaws are fallen; death carries away all the goodly spoil of beauty. It changes a living body, into a foul carcass...Take a body of the finest spinning, once death like a moth gets into it, it consumes all the lustre and glory of it. Death puts the body into such a frightful state — that nothing can desire it but worms!"

The reality is that while we are in the flesh we sometimes think that we are exceedingly beautiful because of our physical features. However, if we were to compare our earthly, "corruptible" bodies to the beauty of all things heavenly, they could hardly compare!

> **The point I am trying to make here is that no matter how good-looking you are in your earthly body, or how complete you are in the flesh, when your spirit leaves your body, it would feel like letting a bird fly away after being caged for many years.**

This is the reason we are repeatedly admonished by the Scriptures to watch over our souls which will endure for all eternity, rather than paying undue attention to our physical bodies. Regardless of the damage and decay our earthly bodies suffer in the course of fulfilling our callings on earth and safeguarding our souls towards eternity, we will be clothed anew with glorious, heavenly bodies in due time.

Author and poet, Horatius Bonar, in comparing our physical bodies with our glorified bodies in death, wrote in the piece, *Coming of the Perfect, Departure of the Imperfect:* "Our flesh, from the cradle to the tomb, is feeble, broken, ready to faint--the cause and the inlet of a thousand sorrows! It is truly a frail body, in which we groan, being burdened; a vile body, needing such perpetual care, and food, and medicine, and rest--yet, after all, incapable of being preserved--which, in spite of all our pamperings, is hastening on to the sick-bed, and the separation from its guest, the soul. But look beyond the tomb and see the glory! This head shall ache no more! These hands and feet shall be weary no more! This flesh shall throb with anguish no more! God Himself shall wipe away all tears from these eyes--and there shall be no more death, nor sorrow, nor crying!"

This calls us to wisdom as Christians. We must be wise in getting our priorities right. It is our souls that matter, not our bodies! Ebenezer Erskine, a Scottish minister also said, "Remember, that whatever care you take about this clay tabernacle, it will drop down to dust before long, and the abhorrent grave will be its habitation, where worms and corruption will prey upon the fairest face and purest complexion. Where will be your beauty, strength, and fine attire, when the curtains of the grave are drawn about you?"

THE ELDERS' PERSPECTIVE

The great saints of old apparently had a better grasp of this truth, which made them have a better perspective of death than most of us in this generation. Paul the Apostle, for instance, once said,

> "For we know that the whole creation groans and labors with birth pangs together until now. Not only that, but we also who have the firstfruits of the Spirit, even we ourselves groan within ourselves, eagerly waiting for the adoption, the redemption of our body"
> **(Romans 8:22-23).**

To the Corinthians, he was even more, explicit:

> "For we know that if our earthly house, this tent, is destroyed, we have a building from God, a house not made with hands, eternal in the heavens. For in this we groan, earnestly desiring to be clothed with our habitation which is from heaven…We are confident, yes, well pleased rather to be absent from the body and to be present with the Lord"
> **(2 Corinthians 5:1-8).**

This obviously was the case with Dr Myles Munroe. His somewhat violent death could be seen as a reflection of the intense desire of his spirit to be liberated from the limiting confinement of his body. Moreover, God never promised anyone that they would die peacefully, in ideal conditions, surrounded by family members.

Even more significant is the fact that Dr Munroe, like most discerning Christians, was fully aware of the possibility of sudden and tragic death, even for believers; hence he advocated the need for thoughtful living. For instance, during one of his final messages shortly before his death, he had challenged the audience in the television studio where the recording was done to think about what would happen to their legacy if they suddenly died in an accident after leaving the studio:

THE FREEDOM OF DEATH

"... If you die today as a leader, leaving the studio in an accident, what happens to your organisation? What happens to your church? What happens to your business? If it dies when you die, you are a failure!"

I definitely don't agree with the assumption that the death of Dr Munroe was as a result of him having done something wrong or that he was in sin or false doctrine.

Having known Dr Munroe personally, I am certain that he lived a full life and accomplished a great work. And even now that he has gone to receive his eternal reward, his departure and legacies continue to stir up others to unleash their potentials for the glory of God.

THE "UNDERAGE" QUESTION

Now, there are also people who have been saying, "If you claim that Dr Myles lived a full life, what do you say about his youth pastor who also died in the crash? What do you say about the youth pastor's son who was only five years old? What about the other people on board that plane? Did they live a full life too?"

I will fully handle this query under the chapter, "STILL WHY DIE SO YOUNG?" However, let me say a few things on it now. Why would God allow the lives of some people to be taken so early? I, of course, cannot say that I have full understanding of the mind of God on the subject, but I hope that some of my explanations will bring peace and solace to people who are sincerely seeking to understand why God would allow something like this to happen to Christians.

One perspective is that death is going to come to us all anyway.

Every individual eventually needs to go home, and to be set free from his or her earthly body, one way or the other. Think of it like being in a prison all of your life and finally being set free from that prison of a body! It really doesn't matter whether God uses this way or that to open the heavenly door for you. For the person who is dead, they're simply glad to be out of that prison!

Indeed, it is needless sympathising with the dead in Christ as if something tragic had happened to them. The truth is that where they are in heaven, they know that we that are still here are the ones who deserve pity for our many battles and vicissitudes. We should not sorrow about them, but instead think about our lives – how we should live so we can be reunited with them in heaven eventually.

Of believers who are gone to heaven ahead of us, First Anglican Bishop of Liverpool, J.C. Ryle in his writing, *Christ's Greatest Trophy!* said, "We should not weep for them, but for ourselves! We are still warring, but they are at peace! We are labouring, but they are at rest! We are watching, but they are sleeping! We are wearing our spiritual armour, but they have forever put it off! We are at sea, but they are safe in harbour! We have tears, but they have joy! We are strangers and pilgrims, but they are at home! Surely, better are the "dead in Christ", than the living! Surely the very hour the poor saint dies - he is at once higher and happier than the happiest upon earth!"

There is no sorrow in death, which is the passageway to believer's home. Heaven is our home. Heaven is our liberty. Heaven is our victory. It doesn't matter how we leave this earth, we are going HOME – and that's what matters!

DEATH'S DEFEAT

The scriptures further promise us that death and the grave would not have the victory over our lives. They do not have the last word; God does!

> "Death is swallowed up in victory. O death, where is thy sting? O grave, where is thy victory?"
> **(1 Corinthians 15:54-55)**

I have heard from people saying that God must have killed Dr Munroe or that Satan must have killed him. The truth is that death did not take Dr Myles Munroe – God did. From the above scripture, the Bible affirms to us that death will not have the victory. The final victory belongs to God and the believers, not to death or the grave.

According to Hebrews 2:14, Christ, in His death, swallowed up death. Therefore, I do not submit to the notion that the believer's death is in any way a victory for the enemy. No! Rather, just like Christ in his death, we too in our death and by our death defeat death. I think our death at any age is a victory for the Kingdom of God and a new beginning for the work of God on earth. Let God decide when it is time for each of us to go home to his or her reward. Whenever that time may be, this much is certain: death for us, believers, is victory. It is liberation. It is triumph. It is home-going. It is the way we go to our reward. It is the way for us to receive our trophies!

Even more cheering is the revelation by Jesus Christ concerning Himself in Revelation 1:18: "I am He who lives, and was dead, and behold, I am alive forevermore. Amen. And I have the keys of Hades and of Death."

Christ says He has the keys of death, which means that the door of death can never be opened to any of His children except He allows it. And should He allow a thing like that to happen, it would be that all would certainly be for the good of the believer. Of this truth, Charles Spurgeon clearly wrote:

> "No man can die unless Jesus opens the mystic door of death. It is our consolation that our death is entirely in his hands. In the midst of fever and pestilence, we shall never die until he wills it. In the times of the greatest healthiness, when all the air is balmy, we shall not live a second longer than Jesus has purposed; the place, the circumstance, the exact second of our departure, have all been appointed by him, and settled long ago in love and wisdom. A thousand angels could not hurl us to the grave, nor could a host of cherubim confine us there one moment after Jesus says, "Arise." This is our comfort. We are "immortal until our work is done;" mortal still, but immortal also. Let us never fear death, then, but rather rejoice at the approach of it, since it comes at our dear Bridegroom's bidding! Christ has the key of death, and therefore death to us is no longer a gate of terror."

BEAUTIFUL "TRAGEDY"

Indeed, it is more tragic if a 90-year-old person dies quietly in his or her sleep, without being saved; or even if he was saved but living for the things of the world. On the other hand, when a teenager dies in an automobile crash, it is not a tragedy if that teenager was saved and faithfully serving God.

"And we know that all things work together for good to them that love God, to them who are the called according to his purpose."
(Romans 8:28)

Therefore we should "Judge not according to the appearance, but judge righteous judgment." (John 7:24).

History itself has taught us that it does not matter how you leave this world, as long as you live every day of your life in preparation for heaven. This truth was not lost on Susannah Spurgeon, wife of the eloquent clergyman, Charles Spurgeon. Following the death of her husband in 1892, she wrote in her collection of writings, "In Memoriam: A Song of Sighs."

> **Indeed, it is more tragic if a 90-year-old person dies quietly in his or her sleep, without being saved; or even if he was saved but living for the things of the world. On the other hand, when a teenager dies in an automobile crash, it is not a tragedy if that teenager was saved and faithfully serving God.**

Ever since the solemn midnight hour when God took to Himself my most precious treasure, "the desire of my eyes," my loving and dearly-beloved husband—the above inspired words ("With Christ—which is far better!" Philippians 1:23) have been a wellspring of solace and comfort to my desolate heart. In the first anguish of my grief, I wrote them on the "farewell" card, and the palm-branches, which waved over his dead body in token of everlasting victory, bore their grand message of consolation to the thousands of weeping mourners.

Now, as the days go by, and the sense of loss deepens, and is still more acutely realized, the blessed fact set forth by these words comes again with Divine power of healing to my sorrowing soul. It is because it is far better for him to be with Christ—that I can patiently and even cheerfully endure my lonely life. I can sometimes dwell with such joy on the thought of his eternal glory "with Christ," that I forget to sorrow over my own great and unspeakable loss.

A dear friend wrote thus to me, the other day, "Oh, when I think of him, as able to praise his Savior, and preach without fatigue or pain—no longer limping, or leaning on his staff—with no cough, no faintness—no swollen fingers or ankles—away from the fogs and mists; where no heresies distress his heart; when I think of him thus, my heart fairly leaps for joy!"

Here again is another beautiful paradox from the Scripture:

> "A good name is better than precious ointment; and THE DAY OF DEATH THAN THE DAY OF ONE'S BIRTH."
> **(Ecclesiastes 7:1)**

I believe the above scripture is self-explanatory enough. From the other side, and from heaven's perspective, the day of death is seen as being more glorious than the day of one's birth, just like a good name is better than precious ointment. However from this side of heaven, we tend to be sad about the day of death, and glad about the day of birth. Ecclesiastes 7:1 says it is actually supposed be the other way round.

Indeed, what really calls for rejoicing is when you depart this sinful world, not minding what age you are delivered from the evils therein. This is because you are going to your reward, and you are claiming victory over death and being welcomed to your eternal home. Your last day on earth should your best day because death is a rest from the trouble of your labours, afflictions, persecutions, temptation and sorrow.

Tell me, reader, is there anything bad about all this? We must learn to see from God's perspective, and to see how God sees. We must be less sensual and strive to become more spiritual. At the end of the day, God decides when we come into this world and He decides when we leave it!

Before I close this chapter, let me challenge you with the letter a minister of God once wrote to one of his church members grieving over the loss of her godly daughter. Just as many are questioning God over the passage of his servant, Dr Munroe, the woman too had been overwhelmed with grief. Here is what the minister, John Berridge, wrote to her:

> "I received your letter, about the death of your godly daughter—and hope that you will soon learn to bless your Redeemer for snatching her away so speedily. Methinks I see great mercy in the suddenness of her removal; and when your affections have done yearning for her—you will see it too."
>
> O! What is she snatched from? Why, truly, from the plague of an evil heart, a wicked world, and a crafty devil—snatched from all future bitter grief, and from everything which might wound her ear, afflict her eye, or pain her heart!
>
> And what is she snatched to? To a land of everlasting peace, where every inhabitant can say, 'I am no more sick!' No more affliction in the body, no more plague in the heart—but all full of love and full of praise; ever seeing with enraptured eyes, ever blessing with adoring hearts—that dear Lamb who has washed them in His blood, and has now made them kings and priests unto God, forever and ever!

Oh, madam! What would you rather have? Is it not better singing in heaven, 'Worthy is the Lamb who was slain!' —than crying out on earth, 'O wretched woman that I am!'

Is it not better to have your daughter taken to heaven— than to have your heart divided between Christ and her? If she was a silver idol before—might she not prove to be a golden idol afterwards?

She has gone to the most blessed place, and will see you again by and by—never more to part. Had she crossed the sea and gone to Ireland—you would have born it; but now that she is gone to heaven—should this be difficult for you? Strange love is this!

Such behavior in others would not surprise me—but I could almost chasten you for it. And I am sure your daughter would chasten you too, if she was called back but one moment from the glories of heaven—to gratify your fond desires! I cannot soothe you—and I must not flatter you. I am glad the dear creature has gone to heaven before you. Lament, if you please; but glory, glory, glory be to God!"

With this understanding, rather than mourn, I'd rather say concerning Dr Myles Munroe:

Dr Myles, I am proud of you! On behalf of Christians everywhere, we are proud of you! What you have accomplished for the Kingdom of God in this life is what matters. It does not matter how you left this world, but rather, what extraordinary footprint you left in it.

That is the question we should be labouring over - what footprint will we leave in this world? Dr Myles left a wonderful, larger than life footprint and it is going to live forever through his books, messages and concepts. As he often said, "The richest place in the world is the grave yard, or cemetery" and "the greatest tragedy in life is not death, but a life without purpose."

These timeless aphorisms spoken by Dr Munroe now testify and speak louder than anything else! Let's now proceed to fully explore the delightful truths about the early deaths of Christians.

> **Dr Myles, I am proud of you! On behalf of Christians everywhere, we are proud of you! What you have accomplished for the Kingdom of God in this life is what matters. It does not matter how you left this world, but rather, what extraordinary footprint you left in it.**

Chapter 3

STILL, WHY DIE SO YOUNG?

In case you still consider tragic and premature death to be inconsistent with the Christian faith, then ponder on this: Why did many of the early believers die so young? Why did many of them die so tragically, instead of dying quietly and in good old age? Could it be that they were not righteous, prayerful or discerning enough? Or could it be that their deaths caught God unawares?

First, let's consider some examples.

John The Baptist

John the Baptist, who did so much as the forerunner and publicist of Jesus Christ, died brutally and prematurely. Of His life, Jesus openly testified, "Assuredly, I say to you, among those born of women there has not risen one greater than John the Baptist..." (Matthew 11:11). When he was imprisoned by Herod, Jesus was fully aware. Being all-knowing, Jesus was also clearly aware that he was going to be killed. Yet Jesus did nothing to rescue him, until he was eventually beheaded. Was Christ's seeming inaction out of wickedness? Certainly not. (Further explanation will be provided on this in the second part of this chapter).

Stephen

Stephen was described in the Scripture as "a man full of faith and the Holy Spirit" (Acts 6:5). He was a young, vibrant apostle of Christ. Yet, he died in a most gruesome manner. Interestingly, shortly before his horrific death by stoning, he testified to seeing Christ standing at the right hand of God. This shows, beyond any shadow of doubt, that Christ was fully aware of his imminent death. Still, he wasn't prevented from dying. You wonder why?

James

James was one of the disciples with very close attachment to Jesus. He was one of the three men in the "inner circle" of Jesus, the others being Peter and John. Yet, his violent death at the hand of Herod Agrippa who had him beheaded was not averted by divine fiat (Acts 12:1-2). Interestingly, the same Herod who successfully killed James, could not succeed in killing Peter as Peter was miraculously rescued from prison by an angel of God. This shows that God's dealings with His saints are purely based on His prerogatives.

Paul

Paul was one of the most prominent of the early Christians. He was used of God to write more than half of the entire New Testament, consisting of 27 books. He was taken to the third heaven where saw and heard what no other mortal man had perceived (2 Corinthians 12:2). Still, he died a violent death by beheading.

All the other apostles of Jesus (with the exception of one – John the Beloved, who merely survived brutal attacks by divine pre-arrangement) equally died tragic and untimely deaths. Historical records have accounts of them being skinned alive, dragged by horses through the street, crucified, clubbed or stoned to death.

Contemporary Cases

Away from the disciples, many Christians in recent centuries, too, have had their fair share of tragedies. Some were fed to the lions, some were burnt at the stake, while others were cast into drums of hot oil and roasted alive. Indeed, all through the ages, down to the 20th century and even the current century, Christians have been killed by various individuals, groups, and by Islamic, communist or atheistic States.

On June 9, 1945, Dietrich Bonhoeffer, a fervent preacher and staunch opponent of the Nazi Germany's attacks against Jews, was executed by hanging by Hitler's government. He was just 39. In his biography of Bonhoeffer's life, Eberhard Bethge, a student and friend of Bonhoeffer's, wrote down the narration of a man who saw the execution:

> "I saw Pastor Bonhoeffer...kneeling on the floor praying fervently to God. I was most deeply moved by the way this lovable man prayed, so devout and so certain that God heard his prayer. At the place of execution, he again said a short prayer and then climbed the few steps to the gallows, brave and composed. His death ensued after a few seconds. In the almost fifty years that I worked as a doctor, I have hardly ever seen a man die so entirely submissive to the will of God."

Obviously, Bonhoeffer was a devoted Christian but that did not prevent him from a ghastly death.

On January 8, 1956, 29-year-old Jim Elliot and his four of missionary colleagues were killed while trying to establish contact with the Auca Indians in Ecuador (now known as the Waodani people). Jim Elliot, Nate Saint, Ed McCully, Pete Flemming and Roger Youderian had been working to make friendly contact with the Auca tribe which they had seen from the air. They would fly around the area, shouting friendship words in the Auca language through a loud speaker and dropping down gifts in a basket. After three to four months of gift dropping, they decided to make a base and set up shelter at nearby river. Not long after, they all were killed by the same people they were trying to help. Their bodies were found brutally pierced with spears and hacked by machetes.

> As I write now, Islamic fundamentalist groups, under various names, are unleashing terror on Christian individuals, groups and churches all over the world. Many have been brutally killed and many more are awaiting their deaths in various dens and dungeons. Does it mean God is not concerned?

Still, apart from cases of Christians being killed by the ungodly, there are also cases of Christians dying prematurely of diseases and disasters. I read recently in the Charisma magazine about a young minister of God called Benny Benson who died tragically of cancer. Author of the article, J. Lee Grady, who also happened to be a friend of the deceased minister narrated what happened:

"Doctors confirmed only 10 months ago that my

friend Benny Benson had a malignant tumour in his spine. He underwent treatment, but in the end more tumours appeared. Nothing could stop the spread of the disease—not radiation, chemotherapy or surgery. He died on Jan. 31, and I spoke at his memorial service in New Hampshire on Feb. 12.

I still can't believe Benny is gone. More than 500 people attended his funeral. Many of them were college students who had been discipled through Benny's campus outreach, which he carried out with his wife, Cindy. Like so many of Benny's other friends and family members, these students had prayed for Benny to be miraculously healed of the cancer.

But in the end, Benny got the ultimate healing—by stepping into eternity."

So, why does God allow all this, despite His promises of long life for His children?

UNDERSTANDING BIBLICAL PROMISES OF LONG LIFE

I have observed over the years that one of the reasons many Christians find it difficult to grapple with tragic and untimely deaths of other Christians is the seeming discrepancy of such occurrences with the scriptural promises of long life.

Let's see a few of these promises.

"No one shall suffer miscarriage or be barren in your land; I will fulfil the number of your days."
(Exodus 23:26)

"With long life I will satisfy him, and show him My salvation."
(Psalm 91:16)

"The Lord bless you out of Zion, And may you see the good of Jerusalem all the days of your life. Yes, may you see your children's children. Peace be upon Israel!"
(Psalm 128:5-6)

"My son, do not forget my law, But let your heart keep my commands; For length of days and long life and peace they will add to you."
(Proverbs 3:1-2)

"Honor your father and mother," which is the first commandment with promise: "that it may be well with you and you may live long on the earth."
(Ephesians 6:2-3)

These promises of God are indeed true and dependable. But we have to fully understand and put these promises in context, so we don't get confused.

First, we must ask ourselves, "What is long life?" Or better still, how does God see long life? This needs to be established because I believe that God's ways are indeed different from our ways and His thoughts ours. To a human being, long life may imply living up to 80, 90, or 100 years and above. But is this really God's viewpoint? If so, why did Christ tell His apostles that they would be hated and killed for His name sake? Could God be lying about the promise of long life when Jesus never intervened in the impending death of John the Baptist? Or could there be inconsistency with God when He allowed Stephen, James and several of His apostles to die young? And is that why He still allows many of His followers down the ages to die prematurely?

Or could it be that we are the ones misunderstanding God's

meaning?

Let the Bible answer for us.

1. In the heavenly realm, days and years are not seen the way we see them on earth.

"For a thousand years in Your sight are like yesterday when it is past, and like a watch in the night."
(Psalm 90:4)

"But, beloved, do not forget this one thing, that with the Lord one day is as a thousand years, and a thousand years as one day."
(2 Peter 3:8)

This should be glaring enough for us to consider and understand. God is not being cruel or untruthful about His promise of long life when He decides to take a believer home suddenly. We may think the individual has not lived long enough based on our calculations of time, days and years; but in God's own calculation, it's another thing entirely.

And why should God's calculation not be different from ours? Do humans really have a specific definition of long life? Several billions of people live on the face of the earth and if you ask each of them on how long is long enough to live on earth, the answers will vary significantly! In fact, most people would love to live on and on. You hardly even find someone who thinks he has lived long enough, except if sickness or disease has turned him to a complete invalid. So, why shouldn't God fix and keep to His own schedule in the midst of our fickleness?

2. Long life is life that is long enough to fulfil our assigned number of days.

In the first passage quoted above on the promise of long life,

God categorically says,

> "No one shall suffer miscarriage or be barren in your land; I WILL FULFIL THE NUMBER OF YOUR DAYS."
> **(Exodus 23:26).**

God's definition of long life is plain enough to see in this verse. He says He will fulfil the number of our days. Let's look at two things here. One, this promise is meant for each individual, not the general mass; otherwise it will imply that we all have the same number of days to live, which is not possible. So we understand that each of us has a specific number of days to live on earth. This is what God promises to fulfil, not our whimsical wishes and expectations.

Secondly, if we agree that this "number of your days" is an individual thing, then WHO fixes this number of days for each individual? Obviously it's God! How many days has He assigned to each of us? Nobody knows. He alone can know and decide which number of years is long enough for each individual, based on what He has assigned before we were born!

Prolific author of religious essays, John MacDuff, says something about this in his writing, *A Book for the Bereaved:*

> "Just as the mother knows the best hour to lay her little one in its couch or cradle—undresses it, composes it to rest, sings its lullaby—and the cherub face, lately all smiles, is now locked in quiet repose; so Christ comes to all His children, of whatever age, at His own selected season, and says, "Your hour of rest has arrived. I am to take off the garments of mortality. Come! I will robe you in the vestments of the tomb." He smooths

the narrow bed, composes the pillow, and sings His own lullaby of love, "Fear not, my child, for I am with you; sleep on now and take your rest!"

Be comforted with this blessed truth, that the hour of death cannot come a moment sooner than Jesus appoints. He knows the best time to bid you and yours the long "good-night." Interesting it is (and a Bible truth too) to think of troops of angels hovering over the death-pillow, and watching with guardian care the sleeping dust of the "Early Grave." But more comforting still, surely, is it to think of the Lord of angels closing the eyes and hushing to slumber—Christ Himself leading to the tomb—the robing-room of immortality—"unclothing," that His people may be "clothed upon," and that "mortality may be swallowed up of life."

3. Long life is life that is long enough to fulfil our purpose on earth.

This is really significant, and this is where I will fulfil the promise I made earlier to explain further about the life of John the Baptist in particular.

God never created a thing without a purpose. This applies even more to human beings, who are created with unique features, talents and traits. To us as humans, all we see in a person are the physical attributes, but God looks far beyond into the specific assignment the individual is created to fulfil on earth. I don't believe anyone is created to simply come and eat, drink, procreate, raise children, enjoy family life and then die. No. So, if there is a unique purpose, an assignment to fulfil, we must ask ourselves, once again, who decides this purpose? Of course, it's God! Who decides when this purpose is satisfactorily fulfilled?

God! Who decides when to recall the individual from his duty-post to give account of His stewardship? It's God!

The challenge with most of us, humans, is that we want God to conform to our own ideas, programmes and perspectives, rather than deciding to ascertain and conform to His. This is why we rush to question God when things don't go the way we think they should go or when people don't live as long as we wish them to.

> "But indeed, O man, who are you to reply against God? Will the thing formed say to him who formed it, "Why have you made me like this?" Does not the potter have power over the clay, from the same lump to make one vessel for honor and another for dishonor?
> **(Romans 9:20-21).**

Now we can apply this explanation to people of God who died prematurely like John the Baptist. What was the mission of John the Baptist on earth? Why did he not live like every other person? Why did he confine himself to the wilderness, eating just locust and wild honey (Matthew 3:4)?

Let's allow him speak for himself. When the Jews sent some priests and Levites to ask for his identity, here's what he said, "I am 'The voice of one crying in the wilderness: "Make straight the way of the Lord,"' as the prophet Isaiah said" (John 1:23)

John's primary purpose on earth, as predicted since the time of Prophet Isaiah, was to be the forerunner of Jesus Christ; he was to prepare the heart of the people for Christ's imminent ministry. Now, did John fulfil that purpose? Obviously yes! Was his life long enough to fulfil it? Yes! Can we say his death was untimely? No.

There are those who think that John might have lived longer

if he had not rebuked Herod for taking his brother's wife. This is an error. When one's assignment on earth is over, one will have to go, one way or the other.

> **Still, on fulfilment of purpose, we must be equally reminded that God does not look at length of life the way we do, nor does He need to inform or consult us when someone's mission is over. What this means is that a person's mission on earth could be fulfilled in one day (as in the case of an infant) or in a hundred years.**

Let me quickly cite two examples.

When David and Bathsheba committed adultery, the whole affair could have been concealed; but God decided to introduce a twist to it – a child was conceived. Why was the child conceived? To expose what was meant to be concealed; to bring the adulterers to penitence and repentance. When David still went ahead to try and cover up his sin by killing Uriah, Bathsheba's husband, God ensured that the child fulfilled its mission.

Note that the child could have died in the womb as a punishment for what David and Bathsheba did; but God allowed the child to be born so David would have developed a strong emotional bond – which would be painfully severed. Nathan, in pronouncing judgement on David said the child would die. Thus, the child was struck with an infirmity. David who had become fond of him could not bear it. He was in such agony that he could not eat for days until the child died (See 2 Samuel 11 and 12 for the story).

Now, to an outsider who never knew what transpired and led to the death of the child, it would seem God was wicked – as some often say today – for allowing the child to suffer and die. It would seem as if the child died too soon. But they err. That child, though still an infant, fully fulfilled his purpose on earth.

The second example I will cite is not about a human being directly, but I believe it will equally help us to better understand the first example, as well as one of God's ways of dealing with us as humans.

When Jonah felt displeased that God had shown mercy to Nineveh following their repentance, God did something extraordinary. He made a tree to grow suddenly so Jonah could hide under its shade. Jonah had thought the tree was going to last for long, but in the original programme of God, it was to fulfil its purpose within a short time. Thus, as Jonah began to feel comfortable, God caused the tree to die. Thereafter, as Jonah complained bitterly about the death of the tree forgetting that it was not his making in the first place, God proceeded to let him know that it was all done for a purpose.

> "But the Lord said, "You have had pity on the plant for which you have not labored, nor made it grow, which came up in a night and perished in a night. And should I not pity Nineveh, that great city, in which are more than one hundred and twenty thousand persons who cannot discern between their right hand and their left—and much livestock?"
> **(Jonah 4:10-11)**

Let me use this to further clarify the issue of death of children. It is indeed a very painful and devastating experience to lose a child or young person, as it happened in the crash that killed Dr Myles Munroe. But one truth must not be lost on us, even as we grieve. We grieve because we're humans. In reality, children are gifts from God and as such are His by ownership. This implies that He can decide when is the best time for them to return to Him. Not that He doesn't care about our feelings, but His eternal purpose cannot be subjected to or regulated by our mercurial feelings.

This is the more reason why we should have the right perspective about God and about life in general, as His word reveals. This will help us to understand and cope with many issues of life – including what we may consider tragic and premature deaths.

Let me show you something challenging from the life of someone. On March 7, 1797, Puritan minister, James Meikle, wrote in his piece, *A Periodic Interview with the King of Terrors*: "Our youngest child for some weeks past has been getting teeth, and was seized with a fever. And though sometimes a little better yet the fever returned and cut her off. Yesterday she was interred. Here divine sovereignty is clearly manifested - I am spared for many years, but my pleasant infant is mingled with the dead! In a little while, it will be eternity with us all! Our best wisdom will be to hold a loose grip on every comfort which can perish, and to fasten our grip on eternal things. The more we have our hearts in heaven--the less will the troubles of time distress us!"

What a challenge!

The example of Job, who lived at a time when there was no Bible or any other scriptural resource, should also both encourage and challenge us. Following the news of the loss of his belongings and dear children, here's what he said: "Naked I came from my mother's womb, And naked shall I return there. The Lord gave, and the Lord has taken away; Blessed be the name of the Lord." The Bible further adds that, "In all this Job did not sin nor charge God with wrong" (Job 1:21-22).

It is my earnest prayer that the Lord will open our eyes of understanding, so we can see with the eyes of Heaven. God is fully aware of all that happens to every one of His children. The fact that He says He is aware of every strand of hair that falls from our heads is enough proof of this (Matthew 10:30). Therefore, it is absolutely clear that God is never caught unawares by the time or manner of His saint's death. He has knowledge and understanding far beyond our comprehension. Only when we acknowledge this fact and resigned to His will at all times and in all situations will we find abundant comfort and solace to cope with seeming tragedies of life

Isn't it refreshing that in hindsight we can see how each one of the early deaths we have mentioned (John the Baptist, Stephen, James, and others) have all come to benefit the Church one way or another today? Yet at the point of occurrence, they looked like tragedies. Without the seeming tragic deaths of these and other martyrs, we would not have had our Christian faith and we would not have had the Church as it is today.

So we can clearly see in all these examples that what we call a "tragedy" might not really be a tragedy in God's eyes. God might just see it as a seed, or an investment! Friend, let me therefore encourage you to look at the events in the lives of our loved ones from God's perspective rather than from our temporary feelings of pain and loss.

Even though I believe we ought to live long, I endorse God's choice whenever He chooses to take any one of His children earlier than we might have expected. I believe such early death could be just as good and beneficial as when someone lives to a ripe old age. Just like we see in the death of the Lord Jesus Christ himself. Therefore, why should we question God in the case of the death of Dr Myles Munroe, his wife, Ruth and the other passengers on that ill-fated flight? Why should we doubt God in this? My understanding is that if God would allow something like this to happen, then according to God's infinite wisdom, it is possibly the best thing that could happen under the circumstances!

> **Even though I believe we ought to live long, I endorse God's choice whenever He chooses to take any one of His children earlier than we might have expected. I believe such early death could be just as good and beneficial as when someone lives to a ripe old age.**

Let me conclude this chapter with the words of wisdom from a letter that a great Bible scholar, A.W. Pink, once wrote to his brother, following the death of a dear one:

> My dear brother,
> My heart goes out to you in sympathy in this dark hour, and I feel my helplessness to comfort you. The loss you have sustained is far greater than any human creature can make up - your suffering is too acute for any fellow-mortal to alleviate. I may endeavour to pour into your sorely-wounded heart something of 'the balm of Gilead,' but only the great Physician can give any efficacy to the same. I can do little more than point you to Him who alone can 'bind up the broken-hearted'. Jesus is a Friend who sticks closer than a brother. Cast all your cares upon Him, for He cares for you. Unburden yourself to Him.
>
> May divine grace be given you, so that you shall be enabled to meekly acquiesce unto whatever our all-wise God may appoint. It is in heart-submission to God's providential dealings with us, that true religion largely consists. Your acute sorrow is among the 'all

things' which work together for good to those who love God. If the Spirit of God is pleased to sanctify this affliction unto you, it will prove a real blessing in disguise. May I suggest several lines of meditation which, if pursued by you and blessed to you by God, will enable you to improve this affliction.

1. Learn anew the terribleness of sin. 'Just as sin entered the world through one man, and death through sin, and in this way death came to all men, because all sinned.' (Romans 5:12) Yes, had sin never entered this world, no graves would have ever been dug in it. Every funeral should be a forceful reminder to us of what the Fall has brought in! Every funeral ought to beget in us a deeper hatred of sin. It was sin which necessitated the death of God's beloved Son. Then how we should loathe it, seek grace to resist its evil solicitations, and follow hard after its opposite--holiness.

2. See the great importance of holding all God's temporal mercies with a light hand. The best of them are only loaned us for a season, and we know not how early we shall be called to relinquish them. It is the part of wisdom for us to recognize and remember this while they are in our hands: not to grasp them too tightly, nor to look upon them as ours to enjoy forever in this perishing world. Holy Writ bids us to 'rejoice with trembling', for that which delights my heart this morning may be taken from me before the shadows of night fall. The more I live with this fact before me, the less shall I feel the loss when it comes!

3. Endeavor to get your heart more weaned from this perishing world. 'Set your affection on things above, not on things on the earth.' (Col. 3:2) But we are slow to heed this exhortation, and often God has to use drastic means to bring us to a compliance with it. It is for our own good as well as His glory, that we do so. It is only heavenly things which abide; then let us seek grace to have our hearts more and more set upon them.

4. Seek to demonstrate the reality of true religion. Only the real child of God is enabled to say, 'The Lord gave, and the Lord has taken away: blessed be the name of the Lord.' Earnestly seek supernatural help from above, dear brother, that you may be enabled to manifest the sufficiency of Divine grace to strengthen and support--to show you do have a peace and comfort which the Christless are strangers to. Sorrow not as others do, who have no hope. Doubt not the Lord's goodness. "Cast your burden on the Lord, and He will support you; He will never allow the righteous to be shaken." Psalm 55:22

Yours by God's abounding mercy,
A. W. Pink

Chapter 4

WHEN DEATH IS GAIN

"For to me, to live is Christ, and to die is gain. But if I live on in the flesh, this will mean fruit from my labor; yet what I shall choose I cannot tell. For I am hard-pressed between the two, having a desire to depart and be with Christ, which is far better"
(Philippians 1:21-23)

What a revelation we have in these verses! What a declaration! To die is GAIN. To depart and be with Christ is FAR BETTER. Paul was simply saying that he was eager to die young, and the only reason he remained behind was for the benefit of those who needed him. He clearly stated that if he had his own choice in the matter, he would rather choose to go to heaven immediately.

What makes one to make such an unusual declaration? It's the power of unusual revelation! Paul the Apostle had seen, through the revelation and assurances of the Spirit of God, that for the believer, it is far better to be dead in the flesh than to be alive. He obviously understood that physical death is not a cessation of life but a transition to a glorious form of life.

Indeed, a right perspective of death will reveal that the pain the bereaved often endures is in no way comparable with the gains that the deceased forever enjoys. People who are afraid of death or who generally have a negative view of it do so because they have little or no knowledge of the purpose it is meant to serve. I'm sure many would actually begin to pray to die, like Paul the Apostle, if they understood that it's actually a sweet experience for the believer. It wouldn't matter when or how it happens; all they would wish for is simply to savour the experience.

Yes, I call death a SWEET experience because, for the believer, death has been disarmed. Praise be to God! Its sting - what should have made it scary and horrible – has been removed by the death and resurrection of Jesus Christ, which gives us hope of resurrection and eternal life.

PERCEPTION OF DEATH IN THE OLD AND NEW TESTAMENTS

Of course, death used to be a dreaded experience for many who lived before Christ came. Several records in the Old Testament attest to this. For instance, the Psalm writer in Psalms 55:4-5 calls death a "terror", saying: "…the terrors of death have fallen upon me. Fearfulness and trembling have come upon me, And horror has overwhelmed me." Job's friend, Bildad, even went further by describing death as the "king of terrors" (Job 18:14).

Then there is the popular case of King Hezekiah, who when told by the prophet of God to prepare for his imminent death, wept bitterly and prayed for more years to live:

"In those days Hezekiah was sick and near death. And Isaiah the prophet, the son of Amoz, went to him and said to him, "Thus says the Lord: 'Set your house in order, for you shall die and not live.'" Then Hezekiah turned his face toward the wall, and prayed to the Lord, 3 and said, "Remember now, O Lord, I pray, how I have walked before You in truth and with a loyal heart, and have done what is good in Your sight." And Hezekiah wept bitterly."
(Isaiah 38:1-2).

Now compare this hysterical reaction of Hezekiah to the news of impending death to that of Paul the Apostle. When it was obvious that his death was near, he became so delighted and expectant. Not even the fact that the death was bound to be violent by way of public execution could dampen his spirits. He wrote to Timothy, one of his mentee-pastors:

"For I am already being poured out as a drink offering, and the time of my departure is at hand. I have fought the good fight, I have finished the race, I have kept the faith. Finally, there is laid up for me the crown of righteousness, which the Lord, the righteous Judge, will give to me on that Day, and not to me only but also to all who have loved His appearing"
(2 Timothy 4:6-8).

What marked the difference between these two men? It was the difference in dispensation. Those in the Old Testament dispensation had limited revelation of the concept of death and the afterlife; while the New Testament, which is rooted in the glorious birth, vicarious death and victorious resurrection of Jesus

Christ, offers deeper and uplifting insight into the experience.

> In this dispensation of grace, all mysteries and uncertainties associated with death have been uprooted. Beyond that, repeated assurances are given throughout the books of the New Testament about the incapacitation of death, leaving the believer with no excuse to cower or sorrow over it.

CHRIST'S PERCEPTION OF DEATH

Jesus gave the most powerful assurance on death when He declared: "whoever lives and believes in Me shall never die" (John 11:26). He did not mean that physical death would not occur to His followers; rather, He wanted to change the perception of the people about death by letting them know that none of His followers would experience death the way the Old Testament people interpreted it to be. He wanted us to see death the way God sees it. He wanted us to know that death, to His followers, should not be a detestable blow, but a desirable blessing.

Presbyterian minister, James Smith, in his writing, *Food for the Soul* used the above comment of Jesus to encourage believers concerning death: "Believer, you have nothing to do with death — for you can never die! For you, Jesus has abolished death, by dying for you, and in your stead. You are in Him, and in Him you may fall asleep — but you shall never die! Death can have no dominion over you."

The disparity between the prevailing perception of death before the coming of Christ, and the perception that Christ wanted the people to have was illustrated in the same John 11. When news came about the death of Lazarus, a beloved friend of Jesus, Jesus did not sorrow or panic. And when he disclosed the news to the disciples, he refrained from using the word "death"; instead, He said, *"Our friend Lazarus sleeps"* (verse 9). Not until the disciples, who had a different notion of death, continued to show that they did not get His meaning did He tell them plainly that Lazarus had died.

Interestingly, this trend of regarding death of the believer as a temporary sleep was subsequently and repeatedly echoed by the apostles in referring to deceased fellow believers following Christ's ascension. Luke, in describing Stephen's death, simply said he fell asleep (Acts 7:60). Paul also repeatedly referred to believers falling asleep in death (1 Thessalonians 4:13-15; 1 Corinthians 15:6, 18, 20). Peter, too, referred to the fathers who fell asleep (2 Peter 3:4).

Commenting on the use of such euphemism by the believers, John MacDuff, said in *Book for the Bereaved*:

> There is no more expressive symbol of higher and diviner verities than the sleep of the body and the subsequent waking in the morning. It is beautiful to see the surging waves of daily life rocking themselves to rest—to note, say, in some vast city, when night has drawn its curtains around, light after light put out in the windows, the street lamps paying solitary homage to the stars as they look down from their lofty mansions. What a hush pervades the recent 'stunning tide of human care and crime!' Why? Because sleep is locking up ten thousand eyes of those who are dreaming away care and sorrow, fatigue and toil. But anon, as the gates of morning open, and when from the silent monitors of fleeting time the hour summoning to labour strikes, in a moment the ring of countless hammers breaks the

trance of night. All is again astir. Sleep has refreshed the workman's wearied body; sleep has put new pith and sinew in that brawny arm. The whole world has arisen like a giant refreshed, and sleep has been the elixir that has soothed its wounds and healed its pains.

OUR VICTORY OVER DEATH

But beyond telling us how we are supposed to view death of the believer, Christ actually went ahead to take the significant step that was meant to liberate us from the torments and terrors of death. He died to conquer the power of death over our lives and minds. Hebrews 2:14-15 says,

> "Inasmuch then as the children have partaken of flesh and blood, He Himself likewise shared in the same, that through death He might destroy him who had the power of death, that is, the devil, and release those who through fear of death were all their lifetime subject to bondage."

Why then do we still continue to glorify death with needless fear? Why do we inadvertently despise the efforts of Christ, the assurances of the scripture and the revelation of the Spirit of God with excessive grief and questions over death of our loved ones? This is unnecessary bondage. The Thessalonian Christians and believers in general were cautioned in 1 Thessalonians 4:13-14:

> "But I do not want you to be ignorant, brethren, concerning those who have fallen asleep, lest you sorrow as others who have no hope. For if we believe

that Jesus died and rose again, even so God will bring with Him those who sleep in Jesus."

Excessive sorrowing over death demeans us as it portrays us as people who are ignorant of their positions and privileges in God's Kingdom; on the other hand, it places us in the same category with the heathen and infidels whose hopes, aspirations and motivations are only confined to this transient world.

Actually, knowing that we cannot do anything about our deceased friends and family members, should be a springboard that should launch us further into the path of wisdom, gratitude and retrospection. We should thank God for the time and opportunity spent with such individuals on earth, and we should strive to fashion our lives after these individuals' faith, especially if they were mentors and leaders who we were particularly impacted by.

The death and resurrection of Christ should equally make us think more deeply. Christ tasted death to make us see that there is nothing horrible about it. I like an illustration that Donald Grey Barnhouse gave about this as he went for the burial of his wife. He said, "I was driving with my children to my wife's funeral where I was to preach the sermon. As we came into one small town there strode down in front of us a truck that came to stop before a red light. It was the biggest truck I ever saw in my life, and the sun was shining on it at just the right angle that took its shadow and spread it across the snow on the field beside it. As the shadow covered that field, I said, "Look children at that truck, and look at its shadow. If you had to be run over, which would you rather be run over by? Would you rather be run over by the truck or by the shadow?" My youngest child said, "The shadow couldn't hurt anybody. That's right," I continued, "and death is a truck, but the shadow is all that ever touches the Christian. The truck ran over the Lord Jesus. Only the shadow is gone over mother."

Even more significant is the resurrection of Jesus Christ which confirms death to be a temporary sleep and also gives us assurance that no believer will be held by the grave forever. In a short while, all the dead in Christ will rise again! As the Scripture says:

> "Behold, I tell you a mystery: We shall not all sleep, but we shall all be changed— in a moment, in the twinkling of an eye, at the last trumpet. For the trumpet will sound, and the dead will be raised incorruptible, and we shall be changed. 53 For this corruptible must put on incorruption, and this mortal must put on immortality. So when this corruptible has put on incorruption, and this mortal has put on immortality, then shall be brought to pass the saying that is written: "Death is swallowed up in victory." "O Death, where is your sting? O Hades, where is your victory?"
> **(1 Corinthians 15:51-55).**

Excessive sorrowing over death demeans us as it portrays us as people who are ignorant of their positions and privileges in God's Kingdom; on the other hand, it places us in the same category with the heathen and infidels whose hopes, aspirations and motivations are only confined to this transient world.

ARE WE STRANGERS OR SETTLERS?

Now, there is something that should challenge and stir up believers of today even more. I have pointed out that the

Old Testament dispensation was a period in which very little was known of the mysteries of death and the afterlife. Yet and interestingly, the Scripture records that despite their limited knowledge, some of the people who lived at that time saw the beauty of death with the eyes of faith and actually lived their lives with their gaze constantly on heaven. Such people were never afraid of death because they saw it as a quick passport to the actualisation of their utmost desire in life. The Scripture speaks of these people in glowing terms:

> "These all died in faith, not having received the promises, but having seen them afar off were assured of them, embraced them and confessed that they were strangers and pilgrims on the earth. For those who say such things declare plainly that they seek a homeland. And truly if they had called to mind that country from which they had come out, they would have had opportunity to return. But now they desire a better, that is, a heavenly country. Therefore God is not ashamed to be called their God, for He has prepared a city for them…Others were tortured, not accepting deliverance, that they might obtain a better resurrection. Still others had trial of mocking and scourging, yes, and of chains and imprisonment. They were stoned, they were sawn in two, were tempted, were slain with the sword. They wandered about in sheepskins and goatskins, being destitute, afflicted, tormented— of whom the world was not worthy…" **(Hebrews 11:13-38).**

What was the secret of the amazing lives of these people? Why was God so proud of them that He was not ashamed to be called their God? Their affection was on heaven not on earth. Whatever they did or had on earth, they were ever mindful of what God expected of them, with regards to their focus and affection.

> I think one of the reasons many of us Christians today fear death and sorrow over it excessively is because we're fast losing focus of our calling. It's the same reason we compromise easily – because we fear persecution; we want to have a sense of belonging, acceptance and comfort in the same world that we claim is not our home!

The Bible describes us as strangers and pilgrims (1 Peter 2:11) and tells us emphatically that "If then you were raised with Christ, seek those things which are above, where Christ is, sitting at the right hand of God. Set your mind on things above, not on things on the earth" (Colossians 3:1). This is the calling of God upon our lives. Until we embrace and obey it, we will not have the right perception of death nor enjoy the comfort and assurance that comes with its occurrence.

In summary, from my exploration of the Scriptures (both Old and New Testaments), I have found that true believers consider death to be gainful for the following reasons:

1. It is a gateway to everlasting rest, blessedness and rewards

> "Then I heard a voice from heaven saying to me, "Write: 'Blessed are the dead who die in the Lord from now on.' " "Yes," says the Spirit, "that they may rest from their labours, and their works follow them."
> **(Revelation 14:13).**

Isaiah 3:10 equally assures:

> "Say to the righteous that it shall be well with them,
> for they shall eat the fruit of their doings."

This is why the real believer sees death as more of a friend than a foe, as John MacDuff once noted: At that solemn season (time of death), it shall be well with him! When the last sands of the numbered hour are running out; when his earthly friends will be compelled to leave him; when the cold dews of death will be standing in large drops upon his pallid brow; when every nerve and vein may be racked and wrenched in fearful agonies by the irresistible power of the grim tyrant — even then it shall be well with him! The dying strife will soon be over, and through death's gloomy portals — he will enter upon that blessed state where all is peace and bliss forever!"

2. It is the way to be transformed into our heavenly bodies, free of limitations, infirmities or deformities.

> "But someone will say, "How are the dead raised up? And with what body do they come?" Foolish one, what you sow is not made alive unless it dies…And as we have borne the image of the man of dust, we shall also bear the image of the heavenly Man"
> **(1 Corinthians 15:35-36, 49).**

Thomas Brooks, in his *Words of counsel to a dear dying friend* explains that, "a saint's dying day is the daybreak of eternal glory! In respect of pleasure, peace, safety, company and glory-a believer's dying day is his best day. Look upon death as a remedy, as a cure. Death will perfectly cure you of all bodily and spiritual diseases at once: the infirm body and the defiled soul, the aching head and the unbelieving heart. Death will cure you of all your ailments, aches, diseases, and distempers. In Queen Mary's days, there was a lame Christian, and a blind Christian--both burned at one stake. The lame man, after he was chained, casting away his crutch, bade the blind man to be of good cheer; "For death," says he, "will cure us both; you of your blindness, and me of my lameness!"

3. It is an avenue for blissful reunions and togetherness

The Bible says of the death of Abraham: "Then Abraham breathed his last and died in a good old age…and was gathered to his people." (Genesis 25:8). Who were these people? Could it be his people back in Ur of the Chaldees? Certainly not, because he was buried in Mamre. "His people" were his wife and other saints who had gone before him, as well as the company of heavenly hosts waiting for him. In the New Testament, it is said that we are surrounded by a cloud of witnesses who had gone before us (Hebrews 12:1) and are now cheering us on, and waiting for us to join them in the beautiful city of everlasting lights. These include saved relatives, friends and other fellow Christians who had died before us.

4. Above all, it is an avenue to meet and be with our Saviour forever. As Paul says, "We are confident, yes, well pleased rather to be absent from the body and to be present with the Lord." (2 Corinthians 5:6). This is why C.H Spurgeon once wrote:

> Death gives us infinitely more than he takes away! To stand before that throne upon the sea of glass mingled with fire, to bow within the presence chamber of the

King of kings, gazing into the glory that excels, and to see the King in his beauty, the man that once was slain, wearing many crowns and arrayed in the vesture of his glory, his wounds like sparkling jewels still visible above!

Oh! to cast our crowns at his feet, to lie there and shrink into nothing before the Eternal All, to fly into Jesus' bosom, to behold the beauty of his love, and to taste the kisses of his mouth, to be in Paradise, swallowed up in unutterable joy because taken into the closest, fullest, nearest communion with himself! Would not your soul burst from the body even now to obtain this rapture?"

Chapter 5

FROM EARLY DEATH TO TIMELESS FAME

There is one interesting thing I have observed in history, which further makes me to view early death in a different and more positive light. When leaders die in their prime, they tend to automatically become legends. A legend, according to the dictionary, is "an extremely famous or notorious person, especially in a particular field."

Do you know what is common to Alexander the Great, Napoleon Bonaparte, and Martin Luther Jnr? One, they died young. Two they are considered legends. Now, even though we may not share the mindsets or values of all these individuals, it goes without saying that each of them died in their prime and achieved legendary status. This does not necessarily mean that older people who die do not gain legendary status; the fact still remains that those who die in their prime are not always worse off, as some people think.

Human beings tend to be more fascinated by strength, vigour, energy, beauty, and charisma rather than weakness, weariness, brokenness and old age. For example, in recent American history, both Ronald Reagan and John F. Kennedy were Presidents of the United States. Both were equally great with respect to their track records; however, after JFK died tragically in the prime of his life, he became a legend, towering higher than all of the other presidents to date.

Of course, some historians would argue that there are other American presidents in recent history who have done much more than JFK. Yet, their names are not as renowned and famous. Even though he was only in office for three years, Kennedy truly became a household name. He was the youngest ever person to be elected president of the United States, which means that he was also youngest to have died; still ovations for him continue to resonate louder than for many others.

Now, compare the iconic reputation of JFK to that of Ronald Reagan who was in office for two terms and arguably accomplished much more. Despite his numerous achievements, he does not command the measure of popularity and clout of JFK amongst ordinary people all over the world. Their funerals also were absolutely incomparable. While the whole world stood at attention to celebrate the life of JFK, very few outside the United States were aware of the death and funeral of Ronald Reagan which occurred in a good old age.

The difference? The age and nature of their death! Which means that God does sometimes use early and tragic death to accomplish His purpose.

A similar thing could be said of African American civil rights leaders, Martin Luther King Jr. and Malcolm X. Both of these men died in the struggle for social and racial equality in America. They have now attained legendary status, crossing all racial barriers throughout the nations of the world. But again we know that they were not the only leaders of the civil rights movement in history; yet they were the only ones to have attained such legendary status.

The difference? The age and nature of their death!

If we look into the showbiz and entertainment world, we see a similar trend. Whenever a star or a leader dies young in his or her prime, they are immortalised and almost immediately attain legendary status. For example, the Jamaican reggae artist, Bob Marley is now a legend. The same goes for the renowned king of rock and roll, Elvis Presley, as well as John Lennon of the Beatles, Jimmy Hendrix and an array of others.

The difference? The age and nature of their death!

> **Even though I am not a supporter or believer in the values and life-choices of some of these individuals, as a thorough student of history I cannot deny this consistent pattern and historical trend. I am sure there are other incredibly talented and gifted individuals who died in a good old ripe age and became legends. On the other hand there are others who died young and did not attain such status. Still the trends and pattern continue to suggest that when leaders die in their prime, they tend to become legends.**

Let me make more comparisons. Two great women died in the same week. Both of these women accomplished unbelievable feats in their lifetime. However, while one died a peaceful death in old age, the other died young and tragically. Surprisingly, while the attention of the world was focused on the death of one of the women, only few people managed to hear about the death of the other even though she was perhaps more accomplished than the former. The two women were Mother Theresa of Calcutta and the Princess of Wales, Diana.

The difference? Their ages and nature of their deaths!

DETAILED EXAMPLES

You probably have heard of the Battle of Waterloo. You may have also heard the main gist of the battle: A French army under the command of Napoleon Bonaparte was defeated by an Anglo-allied army under the command of the Duke of Wellington, with help from a Prussian army under the command of Prince Blücher. Simply put, in that battle, Napoleon Bonaparte was the loser and Wellington the winner. But surprisingly, Napoleon is by far more popular than the Duke of Wellington. Despite his loss, he immediately became a legend soon after his early death. On June 16, 2015, the New York Times published an article with the spectacular headline: 200 Years After Waterloo, Napoleon Still Wins by Losing. The article goes on to include a quote by a researcher who said, "In terms of glory and of history, it is Napoleon who stays in people's minds, not Wellington,"

In fact, so ironic is the situation that unlike Napoleon, many do not even know the real name of the Duke (Arthur Wellesley) who lived much longer than Napoleon. He lived up to 83, while Napoleon who was born in the same year with him, died at 52. Interestingly, while Napoleon's life was relatively short, he went on to become one of the most celebrated figures in history. A website dedicated to his life explains the situation thus:

> "The first signs that Bonaparte's death would prove a significant moment in history - one which would fascinate people across the world - came immediately after his post-mortem. The linen that was on the bed during the examination, "though stained with blood", was torn into pieces and given to those in attendance.

This is the first example of people collecting Napoleon memorabilia in an almost fanatical fashion…the amount of Napoleonic memorabilia also increased dramatically after the emperor's death. Just as on St Helena, Napoleon's admirers were eager to collect anything that could be associated with him. Nor was it just his officers, family, and friends who collected these mementos but members of the general public as well. The population realised that the death of the Emperor was a momentous event in time…"

Hundreds of years later, while very little is known about the victorious Duke of Wellington, Napoleon's legendary status continues to soar. As the aforementioned website further notes, "The amount of publications, articles, and essays published in the month after his death was astronomical…Studies of Bonaparte are continually appearing, from paintings, portraits and caricatures to poems and songs, diaries, journals and newspapers; he is forever present."

Let's move further a bit. Did you know that of all the kings that ruled Egypt in the pre-modern era, King Tutankhamun (also known as Tutankhamen and 'King Tut') is probably the most renowned? However, his legendary status only materialised following his tragic death at just 17 years of age. The Ancient History Encyclopaedia in 2014 aptly described him as "the most famous and instantly recognisable Pharaoh in the modern world."

Thousands of years after his reign and life were brutally terminated, quests have been made, books have been written and movies have been shot in a bid to capture the life and death of this juvenile royalty. Yet there were several other pharaohs before and after him who reigned for long and died in old age and the world knows nothing about them. He probably might have gone the same way, had the circumstances surrounding his death been different.

What do we say of Joan of Arc, the heroic woman who led France to a historic victory over the British during the Hundred Years' War? She died in a most tragic way at just age 19: she was burnt at the stake. Following her death however, she became an iconic legend, an undying super-heroine. I like the way the New York Post of July 26, 2015 captured her legendary status:

> Joan of Arc may have died half a millennium ago — but the 19-year-old French maid-turned-military leader has remained an obsession. She's become anything her fans want her to be: A miracle worker, a feminist, a saint.

Another writer said it more succinctly, "Joan of Arc has since become a role model for girls and women everywhere as a woman who conquered seemingly indomitable odds in a world of men. But one must wonder: Would the legend of Saint Joan have the magnificence that it does had Joan not been burned when she was?" Of course, the answer, even though the author obviously expects none, is No.

You may have heard too of Amadeus Wolfgang Mozart, the prolific and influential composer who has continued to bless our world with timeless classical tunes - symphonies, concertos, operas and so on. Mozart died at the age of 35. And since then, his works and life have gained so much attention and popularity globally.

As the Wikipedia rightly notes: "Indeed, in the period immediately after his death, his reputation rose substantially: [there was] an "unprecedented wave of enthusiasm" for his work; biographies were written (first by Schlichtegroll, Niemetschek, and Nissen); and publishers vied to produce complete editions of his works."

MUNROE'S EXPERIENCE

What we have observed from the honour accorded most of the heroic men and women in history who died young also played out in the case of Dr Myles Munroe. In the hours following his death, there was outpouring of condolences from all nations of the world as most of the top media outlets of the world covered the news.

In fact, for some days, social media majored on nothing else but the death of the humble preacher from one of the smallest nations of the world. Moreover, YouTube views of Dr Munroe's messages and sermons after his death skyrocketed several times over. Many people who had not paid attention to him while he was alive started buying his books, and listening to his messages – bringing the light of the gospel to the dark places of the earth. Dr. Munroe's books and materials also increased in sales at an astonishing rate leading many to believe that in death he may have reached more people than he did in his lifetime.

> **I am not trying to say that fame and legendary status is the ultimate assessment of the value of our life on earth, but as believers, real influence on our world ought to be our paramount objective. When the whole world talks about the death of one Dr Myles Munroe it has a ripple effect on the gospel throughout the world.**

Again, I'm not trying to establish a doctrine regarding the advantages of dying young, or in your prime. What I am saying is that however long God permits you to live on this earth, it is for a reason. So, while living up to 70 or 80 years old could be a good thing, at the same time, someone passing away young could also be a good thing! In either case, God could choose to glorify Himself in the manner of life or death of his children. Let's take a look at Acts 21:13:

> "Then Paul answered, what mean ye to weep and to break mine heart? For I am ready not to be bound only, but also to die at Jerusalem for the name of the Lord Jesus."

Paul, as we have noted in the previous chapter, never saw death as a tragedy. He saw death as a victory! There is no question about that. The most important thing for Paul was that his death or life would glorify the Master. So the question of age or length of life should not be a point of contention at all. This goes a long way in affirming the statement of Dr. Myles Munroe when he said, "Life is not measured by its duration, but by its contribution."

Moreover, it is often said that the "blood of the martyrs is the seed of the Church." In the Early Church, Christians believed that it was to the advantage of the Church when they were martyred because through their death, the Church grew in grace and influence.

Again, let me emphasise that I am not propagating any new doctrine; I am only trying to reveal to us that whatever God does is always GOOD even if we don't understand it. I am also not trying to allude to the fact that Dr. Myles Munroe is a martyr by any means; rather, my focus is on people who die young and tragic deaths.

Chapter 6

DYING EMPTY: A MORE NOBLE CONCERN

American Civil War leader, Stonewall Jackson, was once asked how he was able to display extraordinary calm and courage on the battlefield, despite constant threats of death. He replied:

> "God knows the time for my death. I do not concern myself about that, but to be always ready, no matter where it may overtake me. That is the way all men should live, and then all would be equally brave."

I fully agree with this profoundly wise view of life. Indeed, one of my personal beliefs about life and living is that the greatest enemy of man is not death in itself, but the fear to live. Put more simply, there are people who are so terrified of dying that they never actually begin to live. To live in this context is to fully explore and fulfil one's purpose of being created in the first place. God has a special purpose for creating each person and I believe that death is not the worst tragedy that can befall anyone as many think. The worst tragedy in life and eternity is not fulfilling the purpose of being born.

It was Stephen Vincent Benét who once said that "Life is not lost by dying; life is lost minute by minute, day by dragging day, in all the thousand small uncaring ways." What this means is that it is not really death that robs many people of living a full and fulfilled life. What robs them of such enviable life is their personal choice to live a life without purpose, focus, vision or passion.

> **The truth I am trying to unveil and establish here is that a person could seem to be enjoying longevity of life to the ordinary eyes but, in reality, the person is as good as dead. A person could seem to be full of life, energy and even wealth, whereas in the spiritual realm, he or she is actually seen as a walking corpse.**

Christ said something grim to the Church in Sardis, which sadly, still applies to many lives today: *"You have a name that you are alive, but you are dead."* (Revelation 3:1). This verdict from the mouth of the Lord Himself should set us thinking: Of what use is living up to a hundred or even a thousand years on earth when each day of those plentiful years is not spent pursuing or fulfilling God's preordained will for such an individual? The Bible has it that Methuselah lived for 969 years and procreated. But what else was written of him throughout the Scriptures that was significant? Nothing! Whereas, Moses lived for 120 years and records of his exploits adorned both the Old and the New Testaments. In fact, even after death, his exploits continued as he was one of those who conversed with Christ at His transfiguration!

Personally, I have seen many Christians live unproductive lives because they've got their priorities and preoccupations wrong.

Rather than reflecting on the many opportunities they have to make their destinies glorious and their legacies indelible, they choose to be burdened by the adversities of life and overwhelmed by the cruelties of death. With this mentality, it becomes so difficult for them to maximise their potentials and actualise their destinies. And by the time death eventually comes, it takes them away with all their gifts and capabilities, and they leave the world without any significant contribution to it.

It is of this set of people that Mark Twain, the celebrated author and humourist, said shortly before his death in 1910:

> "A myriad of men are born; they labour and sweat and struggle; they squabble and scold and fight; they scramble for little mean advantages over each other; age creeps upon them; infirmities follow; those they love are taken from them, and the joy of life is turned to aching grief. Death comes at last – the only unpoisoned gift earth ever had for them – and they vanish from a world where they were of no consequence, a world which will lament them a day and forget them forever."

Oliver Wendell Holmes' view of such people is even more direct and poignant. He wrote: "Alas for those that never sing, But die with all their music in them."

What a tragedy! I pray for you that this never happens to you because, as Og Mandino, once wrote, "Hell begins the day that God shows you all that you might have accomplished which you did not."

But we all must go beyond prayer and take a vital decision. That decision is the focus of this chapter. It involves changing our preoccupation from worrying about death, to making the most of our lives so that whenever and however death comes, we shall, in the words of Dr. Myles Munroe, die empty. Yes, die totally EMPTY!

WHAT DOES IT MEAN TO DIE EMPTY?

Dying empty doesn't mean you are devoid of content or vision but rather that you would fully release the vision and the content of your calling for the next generation to run with. To die empty is to die without the baggage of untapped potentials, unfulfilled callings, undeveloped abilities, and even unresolved grievances. It means dying without leaving anything undone which should have been done. It means dying with a sense of confidence and fulfilment that we executed the exact purpose for which we were created.

Of course if Dr. Myles Munroe were to live another hundred years he would have always had something to say, but even at the age of sixty when he died we can all testify to the fact that we have all heard his message clearly. He had truly spoken loudly and had fully released his message to the earth to consume!

Irish playwright and co-founder of the London School of Economics, George Bernard Shaw, captured the meaning of dying empty when he said, "I want to be thoroughly used up when I die, for the harder I work the more I live. I rejoice in life for its own sake. Life is no 'brief candle' to me. It is sort of a splendid torch which I have got hold of for the moment, and I want to make it burn as brightly as possible before handing it on to future generations."

Todd Henry who wrote the book, "The Accidental Creative: How To Be Brilliant at a Moment's Notice" once shared a personal experience with clarifying insight on the subject of dying empty. Here it is in his words:

> "Several years ago I went through a fairly significant examination of life, work, family, art and where it all was headed. I had just ended a pretty intense season in which I found myself spread thin and a little over-extended, and I knew that I couldn't sustain the pace indefinitely. Still, it was a critical juncture in my life and career. I was looking for some insight on how to stay engaged and keep moving forward.
>
> During that season, I was in a meeting in which a South African friend asked, "Do you know what the most valuable land in the world is?" The rest of us were thinking, "Well, probably the diamond mines of Africa, or maybe the oil fields of the middle east?"
>
> No, our friend replied, it's the graveyard, because with all of those people are buried unfulfilled dreams, unwritten novels, masterpieces not created, businesses not started, relationships not reconciled. THAT is the most valuable land in the world.
>
> Then a little phrase popped into my head in such a way that it felt almost like a mandate. The phrase was "die empty." While it may sound intimidating, it was actually very freeing because I was suddenly aware that it's not my job to control the path of my career or what impact I may or may not have on the world. My only job—each and every day—is to empty myself, to do my daily work, and to try as much as possible to

leave nothing unspoken, uncreated, unwritten.

I made a commitment that if any given day were my last I wanted to die empty, having completely divested myself of whatever insight or work was in me to share on that day. As I began to apply this principle to relationships, art and work, I felt a measure of peace even in the midst of busy times. Once I realized that I only have influence over the work that's in front of me, I stopped trying to control things that were beyond my grasp.

I still have long-term goals, and I think they're essential. (I just checked one off my list by publishing my first book!) But long-term goals can become paralyzing if we fail to realize that we accomplish them one day at a time, or more precisely one decision at a time, as we choose to engage in the work in front of us. Novels, businesses, and masterpieces are nothing more than a collection of choices someone made to empty themselves each and every day. The creative process is a daily assault on the beachhead of apathy."

This is exactly the kind of emancipating revelation and mindset that God expects every one of us to have. If we adopt this approach to life, we will, like Mr Todd, automatically become more thoughtful, more focused, more enthusiastic, more motivated, more disciplined, more judicious, and more proactive. Above all, we become less concerned about ephemeral issues such as death and fleshly cravings and rather be more galvanised towards doing the will of God and fulfilling our destinies on earth.

C.S. Lewis once said, "If you read history you will find that the Christians who did the most for the present world were just those who thought most of the next. It is since Christians have largely ceased to think of the other world that they have become so ineffective in this."

> **Dying empty doesn't mean you are devoid of content or vision but rather that you would fully release the vision and the content of your calling for the next generation to run with. To die empty is to die without the baggage of untapped potentials, unfulfilled callings, undeveloped abilities, and even unresolved grievances.**

The Psalmist says in Psalm 90:12, "So teach us to number our days, That we may gain a heart of wisdom." Our days on earth are finite and limited. And once we gain the understanding that the real danger in death lies in dying with all that God has deposited in us to glorify His name and bless the world, we will be more inclined to gain a heart of wisdom and live our lives with purpose. Our case will be like that of Barzillai the Gileadite, who when invited to Jerusalem by King David to come and live a life of pleasure and enjoyment, simply replied: "How long have I to live, that I should go up with the king to Jerusalem?" (2 Samuel 19:34)

The man was so concerned about the brevity of life that he determined to set his priorities right. He knew that what he needed to be concerned about was not transient enjoyment, but what he would be doing with the remainder of his days of earth. That's what I call purposefulness. It was Og Mandino again who once said that "I am here for a purpose and that purpose is to grow into a mountain, not to shrink to a grain of sand. Henceforth will I apply ALL my efforts to become the highest mountain of all and I will strain my potential until it cries for mercy."

SCRIPTURAL EXAMPLES

In no one is this purposeful living with the goal of dying empty more exemplified than Jesus Christ, our Lord Himself. Knowing fully that He was on earth for a particular purpose which was to liberate mankind from the works of Satan, He was fully determined, in all He did, to ensure that His purpose was fulfilled in all its ramifications. This was why the last words He uttered before His death was: "IT IS FINISHED" (John 19:30). He died empty – giving up the last drop of His blood to fulfil His mission of redeeming humanity

How did He achieve the feat? He made His purpose the PRIORITY of His life. And as I mentioned earlier, once this happens, other events of life, including bereavement, become less significant. Why did Jesus not waste time mourning the loss of His dear cousin, John the Baptist? Why was He not bothered by the occasional character flaws of His disciples, the betrayal of Judas or the denial of Peter? Why did He not listen to James and John's suggestion that He should out of provocation call down fire on an entire city? His gaze was on His goal on earth.

At a time, when He was carrying out part of His assignment on earth, he emphasised clearly to His disciples the reason he seemed so focused on fulfilling His purpose before leaving the world. In John 9:4, He says "I must work the works of Him who sent Me while it is day; the night is coming when no one can work."

Now this is both interesting and instructive. It is interesting because it shows that Jesus Christ knew and admitted that the stages of human existence have both day and night. The day signifies the best moment when opportunities abound with equal abilities to maximise them, while the night represents the time when opportunities will no longer be available – the time of death being very much relevant and applicable here.

Christ's utterance is also instructive because we see what His focus was, and what He expects our focus should be. He didn't allow thoughts of the coming night to bother Him; instead He concentrated His focus, energy and zeal on making the best of the day and maximising the several opportunities it presented. And no wonder that when the night came for Him on the cross, He was confident that all that was necessary had been done. He was sure that He had been completely emptied. And thus, he declared, "IT IS FINISHED!"

I like the commentary of the great theologian, James Sidlow Baxter, on this declaration of Christ. He explained that, "surely, when our Lord exclaimed, "It is finished", He meant that He had now finished the work which the Father had given Him to do. The cry, "It is finished", was the rejoicing, even amid anguish, of the perfect Servant. Glance back to His earlier public ministry. In John 4:34, He says, "My meat is to do the will of Him that sent Me". That was His master-passion…On His way to Gethsemane and Calvary, we find Him saying in prayer to the Father, "I have glorified Thee on the earth. I have finished the work which thou gavest Me to do" (John 17:4)

Let's look again at the life of Paul the Apostle too. What made him totally undaunted and indeed excited about the thought of death? What made him confidently declare, in reference to his imminent death: "For I am already being poured out as a drink offering, and the time of my departure is at hand" (2 Timothy 4:6)? It was because he lived in such a way that He could die empty. Here is how he put it himself: "I have fought the good fight, I HAVE FINISHED THE RACE, I have kept the faith." (Verse 7).

How could a man be so sure He had done all that was expected of Him to do on earth? It's because He spent EVERY DAY of his life doing just that. Like Christ, he seemed to know that he would not always be available or able to do what he was doing. Thus instead of bothering about the brevity of life or the possibility of untimely or tragic death, he spent every available opportunity fulfilling his purpose. From the moment he discovered what it was he was to do, he did it with all his might. He once boldly declared before King Agrippa his attitude towards his purpose: "Therefore, King Agrippa, I was not disobedient to the heavenly vision" (Acts 26:19). How then would such a man be worried or scared about death? He gave himself every day to what he was called to do, regardless of situation, environment or circumstance, until he was totally emptied.

This goes a long way in affirming the statement of Dr. Myles Munroe when he said, "Life is not measured by its duration, but by its donation." What he meant was that it's not about how long we live but the legacies we leave behind.

CONTEMPORARY EXAMPLES

I have other records of believers who were never bothered about the thought of death or dying simply because they were either more focused on what they were called to do on earth or because they were glad they had daily lived to emptied themselves in fulfilling their purposes. Interestingly, some of these people were to die as martyrs in the most horrible way. Yet they were filled with joy and anticipated death as one would welcome a friend bringing relief and consolation.

On Thursday, December 21, 1899, after cutting short a Kansas City crusade and returning home in ill health, American evangelist and publisher, D. L. Moody told his family, "I'm not discouraged. I want to live as long as I am useful, but when my work is done I want to be up and off." The next day Moody awakened after a restless night. In careful, measured words he said, "Earth recedes, Heaven opens before me!" His son, Will, concluded his father was dreaming. But Moody gladly replied, "No, this is no dream, Will. It is beautiful. It is like a trance. If this is death, it is sweet. There is no valley here. God is calling me, and I must go." He died soon after.

Michael Green, in the book, *Running from Reality* tells the story of Herman Lange, a German Christian who was to be executed by the Nazis during the Second World War. In his cell on the night before he was to be killed, Lange wrote a note to his parents. He said two feelings occupied his mind: "I am, first, in a joyous mood, and second filled with great anticipation." Then he made this beautiful affirmation: "In Christ I have put my faith, and precisely today I have faith in Him more firmly than ever." Finally he urged his parents to read the New Testament for comfort: "Look where you will, everywhere you will find jubilation over the grace that makes us children of God. What can befall a child of God? Of what should I be afraid? On the contrary, rejoice!"

This was a young man dying without regrets. The reason? He had no baggage of unfulfilled purpose in life. He was plunged into a situation that should have made many despairing and despondent; rather he was jubilant and triumphant because he had spent his life emptying himself for the cause he was called into.

John Calvin was another man whose approached to death reflected the preoccupation of his life. In his final letter to his old friend William Farel, he wrote:

> "Since it is God's will that you should outlive me, remember our friendship. It was useful to God's Church and its fruits await us in heaven. I do not want

you to tire yourself on my account. I draw my breath with difficulty and expect each moment to breathe my last. It is enough that I live and die for Christ, who is to all his followers a gain both in life and in death."

Here again was another man who could not be shaken by the prospects of death, simply because he had found and stuck to his purpose in life. Interestingly, if there was anyone who should have lived an unfulfilled life occasioned by the reality and possibility of untimely death, it was John Calvin. Why? Because the major part of his 55 years on earth were spent battling one debilitating ailment or the other. Yet, he ensured that whatever little moment of strength and respite he had, he used it maximally and productively. Writing of his struggles, Sam Storms said in the article, *To Live and Die for Christ: Remembering the Death of John Calvin*:

"Calvin's afflictions read like a medical journal. He suffered from painful stomach cramps, intestinal influenza, and recurring migraine headaches. He was subject to a persistent onslaught of fevers that would often lay him up for weeks at a time. He experienced problems with his trachea, in addition to pleurisy, gout, and colic. He suffered from haemorrhoids that were often aggravated by an internal abscess that would not heal. He had severe arthritis and acute pain in his knees, calves, and feet. Other maladies included nephritis (acute, chronic inflammation of the kidney caused by infection), gallstones, and kidney stones. He once passed a kidney stone so large that it tore the urinary canal and led to excessive bleeding."

In all of this, Calvin was never daunted because he was determined to die empty. As Sam Storms further observed, "when he reached the age of 51 it was discovered that he was suffering from pulmonary tuberculosis, which ultimately proved fatal. Much of his study and writing was done while bed-ridden. In the final few years of his life he had to be carried to work"

At a time when his friends expressed concern about his hectic schedule, his replied to them was, "What! Would you have the Lord find me idle when he comes?" He preached his last sermon on February 6, 1564. He had to be carried to and from the pulpit. He lived purposefully until he was totally emptied.

Let me also present an excerpt from a letter by Christopher Love, Welsh Protestant preacher, to his wife, on the morning of his execution for by the British government.

> My most gracious beloved, I am now going from a prison to a palace! I have finished my work. I am now to receive my wages. I am going to heaven! Rejoice in my joy. The joy of the Lord is my strength. O, let it be yours also! Dear wife, farewell! I will call you wife no more! I shall see your face no more! Yet I am not much troubled; for now I am going to meet the Bridegroom, the Lord Jesus Christ, to whom I shall be eternally married! Your dying, yet most affectionate friend until death,
> **Christopher Love,**
> *August 22, 1651, the day of my glorification!*

Why was he so restful in the face of brutal death? Purposeful living. He had nothing to fear.

A WORD OF CAUTION

Now, please don't get me wrong on the subject of emptying yourself before you die. It doesn't mean working perilously without resting or having time for family or some measure of luxury. On the contrary, what it means is that in the midst of the hustle-bustle of the world, you make it a duty to find out God's SPECIFIC purpose for your life and live everyday fulfilling it to the best of your ability.

Dying empty simply entails making every day of your life count in fulfilling your calling. It implies making it your number one focus, amidst every other thing you have to do. So, I am not necessarily saying you must jeopardise your health to live a fulfilled life. My point is that you ensure that you strike a good balance between doggedly fulfilling your purpose and applying wisdom in doing so.

Todd, whom I quoted earlier, offers some clarity on this, in his book, *Die Empty: Unleash Your Best Work Every Day*:

> The phrase "die empty" could easily be misunderstood to mean spending every ounce of yourself on your career...It's not about getting everything done today...Many high-ranking executives have died in the prime of life for no apparent reason other than the ill-effects of overwork. To be clear, this is not what I mean by "die empty." It's not about ignoring all areas of your life so that you can exclusively focus on getting work done. In fact, working frantically is actually counterproductive in many cases. Emptying yourself of your best work isn't just about checking off tasks on your to-do list; it's about making steady, critical progress each day on the projects that matter,

in all areas of life. Embracing work with this mind-set will not only increase your chances of tackling your goals, but will also make it all more gratifying. It's not the same as "live like there's no tomorrow"…It's not about following your whims. You have a responsibility to leverage your passions, skills, and experiences to make a contribution to the world.

Having sufficiently explained the great principle of dying empty, I will now proceed to allow Dr Munroe's voice be heard on the issue.

DR MUNROE'S VIEW ON DYING EMPTY

Here is an extract from one of his sermons, Die Empty:

I was amazed to find that in every place I go in this world…I find the wealthiest place on earth. As a matter of fact, every time I see it I'm reminded "that is it". See, the wealthiest place is not too far from your house. The wealthiest place on earth is not the oil fields of Iraq, Iran, Saudi Arabia or Kuwait. It's not the diamond mines of South Africa, Zimbabwe or the Democratic Republic of Congo. The wealthiest place on earth is the CEMETERY, the graveyard.

You may wonder, why is the graveyard so wealthy? It's because in the cemetery are books that were never written, painting that no wall will ever see; the graveyard is filled with music that no one has ever heard. The cemetery is filled with poetry that no one will ever read, ideas that will never be reality. The cemetery is filled with great men that died as alcoholics and drug addicts; it's filled with powerful women that died as prostitutes; it is filled with dreams that will never come to pass, it is filled with businesses that will never open.

What a tragedy! Every time I pass by, I always think, "If I could mine this place like they do gold I'd be a rich man." For those of you who know me, I am passionate about the youth… every time I see the young I see a candidate to add to the wealth of the cemetery. I can't imagine the cemetery would rob us of the magazine you want to publish, the music you want to produce or the books you want to write.

I want to see the young die empty. I want you to go to the grave yard, young man, young woman finished. I want you to die like Jesus. Go to the grave yard as nothing but an empty carcase. You should not die old but finished. I want you to die like the apostle Paul says, "I have finished my course." Then he says, "I have been poured out like a drink offering, every drop of me is finished. Therefore I am ready to die." You should not die until there is nothing left for you to do. Die empty. That's why God is interested in your life. It's not you that he wants to save; it's what you are carrying!

ADDITIONAL EXCERPT

During an interview in Nairobi Kenya on 24 October 2014, Dr Munroe spoke with former CNN correspondent in Nigeria, Jeff Koinage. He said: "I want to challenge every Kenyan to go to the cemetery and disappoint the graveyard. Die like the Apostle Paul who said I have finished my course, I have kept the faith and I have been poured out like a drink offering. There is nothing left. I am ready to die. That's how I wanna die because there is nothing else for me left to die."

In another breath, he said: "When you die, die like I am planning to die. Empty. It's finished."

Chapter 7

WHERE ARE YOUR TREASURES - HEAVEN OR EARTH?

J.S. Baxter, whom I earlier mentioned, made a vital observation that I consider most apt for the question that constitutes the focus of this chapter. He said:

"Among the generality of people, death is considered the greatest of all losses. That is not to be wondered at. The merely natural man lives only for this earth and this life. His pursuits and pleasures and possessions are all things of this present world. At death he must leave them all. He has invested nothing in this life beyond. Even if he believes in a life beyond, his ideas of it are vague, and he dies unprepared for it. The last few flickers of his earthly pleasures are smothered in a comfortless grave."

The implication of this observation is so deep, illuminating and thought-provoking. But before analysing it, let me compare it to the admonition of Jesus Christ Himself, from which the caption of this chapter was derived. Christ, in Matthew 6:19-21 says:

"Lay not up for yourselves treasures upon earth, where

moth and rust doth corrupt, and where thieves break through and steal: But lay up for yourselves treasures in heaven, where neither moth nor rust doth corrupt, and where thieves do not break through nor steal: For where your treasure is, there will your heart be also."

My primary focus is on the last verse: Where your treasure is, there will your heart be also. Christ here presents both a yardstick for measuring true Christianity, as well as the focus that every true believer ought to pursue. The message he conveys here is one that nobody can dispute: We are often most concerned about where we have the bulk of our treasures.

By the way, what is a treasure? The dictionary defines it as something that is very special, important, or valuable and is usually kept in a safe place.

It is clear then that what Christ is saying is that the state of our heart or the focus our of lives is always determined by the location of the things we consider most important and most valuable to us. In essence, it is the location of our treasures that determines the direction of our lives.

A QUESTION TO ANSWER

So we come back to the question that forms our focus in this chapter. Where are we storing our treasures? Where are the things we value the most as Christians? Or better still, to use Christ's analogy, on what is our heart focused? What is the overruling PASSION of our heart? What controls our daily thoughts, words, actions and interactions? Is it the desire for the things of this world or the attractions of heaven? This is what really determines the depth or even genuineness of the Christianity we claim to practice.

"What a man loves," says Martin Luther, "that is his God. For he carries it in his heart, he goes about with it night and day, he sleeps and wakes with it."

It's as simple as Luther put it. Whatever we value so much that we find so difficult to part with has become our god, the focus of our mind and worship. So, where exactly is our God as Christians? Is our God the god of this world or the one whose throne is in Heaven? The answer lies in the focus of our heart. If, truly, God whose throne is in heaven is our Father; if, truly, Christ who ascended to heaven has become our Saviour and Lord, if the mansions He's gone to prepare are indeed meant for us; if the saints that have gone ahead are truly our fellow brethren; if indeed we had been labouring to win souls into the heavenly kingdom; if indeed we have invested our time, resources and energy for the expansion of the course of heaven, why would we not be eager to go there?

Richard Steele once echoed what many other saints of God have repeatedly affirmed saying, "now though death is an unwelcome messenger to those who live for this poor world — yet to a holy old man and woman, it is a blessed privilege. For as looking backward they see a tempting troublesome world — so looking forward they see a state of perfect holiness and happiness prepared for them. The end of their fight — is the beginning of their victory. As they part from their earthly labors — they take possession of their heavenly honours."

This is how it should be for the true believer, but I'm surprised that the situation is often not so with many of us. This is an irony that never ceases to baffle me. We Christians profess to love the Lord with all our heart, soul and strength, which should naturally infer that we desire to go and be with the One we love. Especially, if we say we love Him more than everything, including life itself. Yet, we are afraid of death. How are you going to be with the

One you love without dying?

If we really love Him as much as we profess to, then going to be with Him would have been our paramount desire in life. The question then arises: Are we sure that we are really in love with Him as we confess to be? Because, with the exception of the rapture, we will all need to die to go be with the Lord. Death therefore should not be a thing or source of fear to the believer; rather it should and must be a source of inspiration, excitement, joy and nostalgia.

> **This is an irony that never ceases to baffle me. We Christians profess to love the Lord with all our heart, soul and strength, which should naturally infer that we desire to go and be with the One we love. Especially, if we say we love Him more than everything, including life itself. Yet, we are afraid of death. How are you going to be with the One you love without dying?**

On the other hand, we believers say we all want to go to heaven. We preach about it, sing about it, pray about it but when it comes to dying which is the only way to get to heaven right now (with the exception of the rapture), we kick against it, we fight and protest instead of rejoicing about the prospect of getting to where we have dreamt about all along. Brethren, let's be real!

I sincerely don't believe that we are hypocrites but I am convinced that most Christians are not being realistic. We must teach our congregations to be more in the here and now, to live in active consciousness and to add to their faith understanding.

Several years ago, when a precious member of the church of the revered minister of God, J.A James died prematurely and many in his congregation were downcast, he wrote the following letter to them:

WHERE ARE YOUR TREASURES - HEAVEN OR EARTH?

In the death of our dear friend Elmore, the church has lost a very valuable member, and I a most affectionate friend. Cut off in the prime of his life—his death speaks loudly to us all. What now is the world, or any of its concerns, to him? Let our hearts be more in heaven! We are too earthly and sensual. We are too much elated by the comforts of life; and too much depressed by the sorrows of life—forgetting how close at hand is the event which will render them both alike indifferent to us—and us to them. Eternity, eternity is before us—and what earthly trifle should greatly affect those who are speedily traveling to eternity?

Speaking of myself, I would say like Paul, that for me to live is Christ and to die is gain. It is my earnest desire to leave this earth as fast as possible and I am not seeing this as a tragedy at all! Living on this earth is not my greatest dream. My dream is to live in heaven.

> **The life I am living on this earth is being driven by my passion to get to heaven. Therefore life on earth is not my motivation. Nothing motivates me on this earth as heaven does. My image of heaven is so clear that I am dreaming and earnestly preparing to go there and I pray that it happens as fast as possible.**

So even though in the meantime I have to remain on earth, it is actually more of a sacrifice for me!

To be honest, whenever I voice this kind of sentiment, people around me get nervous and try to convince me otherwise! However I cannot be convinced otherwise. I think anybody who is dreaming of merely a better life on earth is the one who is mistaken. Even though we are on earth, busy with the work of the Lord, we should not be overly captivated by the desires and pleasures of this earth. I believe that we must keep our focus on heaven and eternity. That is where our passion should be. That is what our vision and goals should be focused on, and that should be the source of our motivation. It is misguided to think that the earth is our ultimate desire. No my friends, heaven is!

C.H. Spurgeon once expressed the same sentiment when he said: "never fear dying, beloved. Dying is the last, but the least matter that a Christian has to be anxious about. Fear living — which is a hard battle to fight, a stern discipline to endure, a rough voyage to undergo."

DANGER OF BEING WORLDLY-MINDED

The real danger in being so fixated by the things of this world that we feel so relaxed and reluctant to leave it for heaven is outlined in the points I explained below. Attachment to the world in any form does the following:

1. It portrays us as people who don't really love God.
Regardless of what we profess, excessive attachment to the world shows that we don't really love God as we claim. 1 John 2:15 says, "Do not love the world or the things in the world. If anyone loves the world, the love of the Father is not in him."

2. It portrays us as belonging to the world, not to God.
Jesus Christ says of those who truly belong to Him. "They are not of the world, just as I am not of the world." (John 17:16). Jesus was never so comfortable in the world because He knew

He was not of the world; He only came to fulfil a mission. He knew that succumbing to the allurements of the world comes at a heavy price – bowing to Satan, the god of this world (Matthew 4). This was why He was not bothered about leaving the world so soon. In fact, when Peter tried to dissuade Him from dying so He could stay longer in the world, He instantly recognised that it was the DEVIL speaking and rebuked him!

This is the same attitude that Christ expects of His true followers. If He could not feel at home in the world because He was not of the world, how could anyone having His nature feel so comfortable in the same world? The temptation to be so relaxed in the world is from the devil who wants to ensnare the believer. So we must be watchful. "If then you were raised with Christ, seek those things which are above, where Christ is, sitting at the right hand of God. Set your mind on things above, not on things on the earth" (Colossians 3:1-2).

It is not by accident that Christians are called "strangers and pilgrims" and "ambassadors for Christ" (2 Corinthians 5:20). No stranger, pilgrim or ambassador feels so comfortable about the place of his temporary abode that he stops longing to return to his homeland. Should this happen, it is a sign that the so-called stranger, pilgrim or ambassador has chosen the foreign land above his home-country because he considers it better. When a Christian begins to prefer to stay back on earth than go to heaven, it is a dangerous sign of adapting and adjusting to the world.

I once read a story about an American tourist's visit to the 19th century Polish rabbi, Hofetz Chaim. Astonished to see that the rabbi's home was only a simple room filled with books, plus a table and a bench, the tourist asked, "Rabbi, where is your furniture?" "Where is yours?" Replied the rabbi. "Mine?" Asked the puzzled American. "But I'm a visitor here. I'm only passing through." "So am I," said Hofetz Chaim.

Action speaks louder than words. Whether we belong to God or the world will be manifested in the way we live our lives and conduct our affairs!

3. It portrays us as enemies of God.

This is a blunt reality, which must jolt us to realigning our focus and priorities as Christians. Apostle James says it unequivocally: "…Do you not know that friendship with the world is enmity with God? Whoever therefore wants to be a friend of the world makes himself an enemy of God." (James 4:4).

The logic in this warning is simple. The closer we get attached to the world, the farther we move away from God.

4. It portrays us as unwise people.

This is another jolting and disconcerting reality. Only unwise people invest in businesses and ventures that are doomed to fail. Only unwise people put all their hard-earned money in a bank that is set to liquidate! Jesus warns us: "Lay not up for yourselves treasures upon earth, where moth and rust doth corrupt, and where thieves break through and steal: But lay up for yourselves treasures in heaven, where neither moth nor rust doth corrupt, and where thieves do not break through nor steal" (Matthew 6:19-20).

The best of our worldly possessions and obsessions are at best temporary and at worst agents of sorrow and discontent. Thomas Brooks, in his writing, *The Golden Key to Open Hidden Treasures* noted that, "Honours, riches, and pleasures are the three deities, which all people adore, and to whom they continually sacrifice their best thoughts and energies. These, for their unparalleled vanity, may well be called "the vanity of vanities!" Honours, riches, and pleasures are but a mere shadow, a vapour, a feather in the cap, a breath, a froth, a dream, a nothing. They are without true substance. Like in a dream, you imagine they have substance—you grasp at them and awake—and they are nothing! And yet, they are the most powerful charm of Satan, whereby he lulls men to sleep in the paradise of fools; to cast them, after they die, into the bottomless pit of eternal woe!"

John MacDuff too, in writing *Ripples in the Twilight* said that, "The world's pleasures are often curses in disguise — like Cleopatra's viper, which was hidden in a basket of flowers. There is often an adder lurking in the bed of roses, a fly in the ointment, poison in the wine-cup!"

5. It can hinder us from making it to heaven at last.

Entering into heaven is never by chance or by accident. It takes conscious desire and preparation. And how can one properly prepare for a place that he is not eager to go? How can one prepare for heaven when he is so comfortable with being on earth?

John Climacus, the seventh-century ascetic who wrote "Ladder of Divine Ascent", was right when he stated, "You cannot pass a day devoutly unless you think of it as your last." No one can be ready for the rapture or heaven or death, whose mind is set on the world. Jesus Christ warns in Luke 21:34: "But take heed to yourselves, lest your hearts be weighed down with carousing, drunkenness, and cares of this life, and that Day come on you unexpectedly." That day could be day of death or the rapture of the saints. Either way, once our hearts are so preoccupied with the cares of this life, we will be caught unprepared.

That was the case with Lot's wife. What made her become a pillar of salt? She looked back at Sodom and Gomorrah, despite divine instructions. Why did she look back? It was obviously because she had become so fond of the city and couldn't bear leaving it so suddenly because her treasures were there! This is why our hearts must be well-guarded as Christians against the invasion of earthly cares and obsessions! We can live and prosper on earth without being attached to it.

I like the way a gospel minister once explained this. According to him, "a true Christian living in the world is like a ship sailing on the ocean. It is not the ship being in the water which will sink it, but the water getting into the ship. So, in like manner, the Christian is not ruined by living in the world, which he must do whilst he remains in the body, but by the world living in him! The world in the heart has ruined millions of immortal souls. How careful is the mariner to guard against leakage, lest the water entering into the vessel should, by imperceptible degrees, cause the vessel to sink; and ought not the Christian to watch and pray, lest Satan and the world should find some unguarded inlet to his heart? "Above all else, guard your heart, for it is the wellspring of life (Proverbs 4:23)."

6. It makes mockery of our religious activities and commitments.

Of what use are our religious activities – church attendance, evangelism, intercessions and the likes – if they are not heaven-focused? What do we gain from contributing to the expansion of God's Kingdom, when we are not mindful of it? What's the point of bearing the name CHRISTIAN, when we are not eager to be finally joined with Christ in heaven?

C.S Lewis once observed that, "We are very shy nowadays of even mentioning Heaven. We are afraid of the jeer about "pie in the sky," and of being told that we are trying to "escape from the duty of making a happy world here and now into dreams of a happy world elsewhere." But either there is "pie in the sky" or there is not. If there is not, then Christianity is false, for this doctrine is woven into its whole fabric."

No wonder, Paul the Apostle emphatically said in 1 Corinthians 15:19: "If in this life only we have hope in Christ, we are of all men the most pitiable."

7. It weakens our commitment and consecration to God's work.

Thoughts of the ultimate joys of getting to heaven and the agonies of missing it are the most powerful forces behind effective soul-winning worldwide. When one is no longer preoccupied by such concerns, it naturally translates into lethargy towards the work of God. Once the vision is lost, the motivation will diminish.

To quote C.S Lewis again, "If you read history you will find that the Christians who did the most for the present world were just those who thought most of the next. It is since Christians have largely ceased to think of the other world that they have become so ineffective in this."

What made Demas, one of the key assistants of Paul, to suddenly forsake the work of God for earthly pursuits? Here is Paul's answer: "for Demas has forsaken me, HAVING LOVED THIS PRESENT WORLD..." (2 Timothy 4:10).

> **Let's be wise and set our focus straight. Heaven is our home. Regardless of the blessings, privileges and opportunities, we have on earth, we must not be carried away to the point of forgetting heaven and jeopardising our chances of getting there.**

Indeed, whether we like it or not, every day of our lives brings us nearer to the appointed time of our exit from the earth. And this is a thought that should make us fix our priorities and focus in the right direction.

J.R Miller gave a beautiful illustration, comparing our days on earth to days in a contracting dungeon!

> There was a mediaeval dungeon of singular construction. When the prisoner first entered it — it seemed very bright and pleasant. It had a cheerful appearance. But in three or four days, he saw that the walls, which were of iron, were slowly contracting. On oiled hinges and in silent grooves, the metal plates were ever drawing nearer and nearer to each other.
> By and by the prisoner could hardly move. Then the place was too small for him to lie down in. The next day, there was only room for him to stand. Now he put his hands frantically against the iron walls to keep them from crushing him. But all was in vain. The walls silently and remorselessly closed upon him.
> In the same way, your years are just like the walls of such a prison. They are bright and beautiful to you. But each day the prison is contracting, its walls are narrowing around you. With every pulse-beat, the iron walls draw closer and closer around your soul.
> The only refuge from this prison, is Christ. Without Christ, life means nothing but illusion and disappointment, ending in death and eternal damnation! Christ is the only door into liberty, into blessedness, into joy, into Heaven!

The joys and attractions of this present world are just for a short while. Soon, they will be gone, and what will happen if we have not taken time to invest our focus, time, energy and resources in heaven?

"Therefore, since all these things will be dissolved,

what manner of persons ought you to be in holy conduct and godliness, looking for and hastening the coming of the day of God…?"
(2 Peter 3:11-12)

Chapter 8

MYLES MUNROE: THE MAN AND HIS MINISTRY

Three days after the passing of Dr Munroe and his wife, his son, Myles Munroe Jnr., spoke on the event at a press conference. During the address, he made this striking remark:

> "We rejoice for we know that they are in a better place watching over all of us and rejoicing among the heavenly angels. We will not allow death to claim any victory, but we will celebrate the life and legacy of each individual."

Indeed, having sufficiently explored the concept of death and its implication for the believer till this point, I will now be dedicating the remaining chapters of this book to celebrating the extraordinary life, ministry and legacies of this departed champion of faith. As we explore all these, I am certain that you, too, will come to the same conclusion as his beloved son, that there is indeed no reason to lament but to rejoice that he was victorious in life and in death.

THE MAKING OF A CHAMPION

Myles Egbert Munroe was born on Saturday April 24, 1954 in Nassau, New Providence Island, in the Bahamas. He was the sixth of eleven children, all raised in a two-bedroom wooden house in Bain Town, one of the poorest parts of the Island.

> **Munroe's family were very familiar with poverty. The children spent their early years sleeping on the floor among rats and cockroaches in their dingy rooms. Despite the squalor that surrounded them, however, the Munroes were fortunate to have a very strong spiritual heritage.**

Both his father and mother knew the Lord and were leaders in their church. Thus, teaching of God's word was constant in their home.

Beyond that, his parents ensured that the children understood the Bible and the essence of a personal relationship with Christ. This was what proved to be the sunshine for them in the shadows of poverty in which they were perpetually subsumed. The scriptural heritage added so much amazing beauty to their world, despite being seen as disadvantaged by many.

When Munroe was five, he began to have divine revelations of the exceptional life he was destined to have. One day, while seated on a heap of dirty clothes, he had a trance. He saw himself as a very successful man, wearing expensive clothes, driving posh cars, and travelling around the world in a private jet. Although too young to understand much of what he saw, he had everything stored in his mind until the fulfilment came.

The indigent condition of Munroe's family obviously affected his early academic life. He was in school on a certain day when a teacher, apparently flustered either by his performance or conduct, told him he was nothing and would never amount to anything in life.

Young Munroe was shattered and disconsolate by the hurtful remark. He ran home weeping and then, falling before his mother, repeated what the teacher had said to him. His vibrant and faith-filled mother immediately quelled the storm of despair raging in him. She held him very close, shook him and said, "First of all, don't you ever say that again." Thereafter, she brought out her big Bible, opened Ephesians 3:20 and instructed him to go into the room and read.

As Munroe read the Scripture, he made the amazing discovery that God's plan for his life totally contradicted what the teacher had said. And that instantly transformed his mood and countenance. The tears disappeared, his face brightened up and he began to laugh with overflowing confidence.

His mother however did not stop at that. One day, having observed that he was spending too much time daily watching television, she told him point-blank: "If you keep watching TV this way, you may never get on TV." The admonition got him thinking and he resolved to substitute the time he was spending watching television with reading books. That decision was later to have a massive impact on his life and ministry.

It was from age 13 that Munroe began to have real personal encounter with God. It all began with the deep sense of curiosity that would eventually make him a living compendium of practical knowledge and ideas about life. From that young age, he began to ask some deep questions about life and the world, questions that most teenagers wouldn't bother to ask. He pondered the existence, goodness and justness of God. If God was real and just as he had been made to believe, why was his family so poor? Why were some people in life basking in prosperity, while others were dying in penury? The fact that, as at then, the Bahamas was under British colonial rule, even made matters worse in his imagination. How could people of a certain race live like royals while those of another race live in subjugation? He gradually began to be embittered about life in general.

Interestingly, it was the Bible again that proved to be His liberator from the shackles of psychological torments. It had helped him before and he decided to turn to it again. By age 14, he had finished reading through the whole Bible. Again, even though he did not understand most of the things he read because he was not yet saved, he set a goal for himself to read through the Bible every year. As he did, his belief systems began to change about himself, about God, about other people, about values, and about moral standards. He also began to align himself with the principles that are laid down in the Bible.

However it wasn't until 1969 at age 15 that Munroe eventually made a definite commitment to serve the Lord. After that he began a gospel musical group, with three of his friends. They wrote their own songs in a way that was contemporary to their time, targeting the youth. However, due to the novelty of their pattern of music, churches in the community would not allow them sing before their congregations. So, they began to organise gospel concerts, all over the Bahamas, using school halls.

Within a short time, Munroe and his group had become so popular that they began to have up to 4000 youth attending their concerts. In fact, by the time he was 17, the group had become the biggest teenage ministry in the country, with one of their songs becoming a chartbuster.

One day in 1972, the then Prime Minister of the Bahamas,

The Right Honourable Sir Lynden Oscar Pindling, informed Munroe's parents that he was eager to have a discussion with their son. When Munroe got to the office of the PM, the PM told him he had been curious to meet him, seeing he had become the most influential person around, even more influential than he, the PM! Flabbergasted, Munroe asked him why he would say that and the PM replied that if he could succeed in getting as many as 4000 youth to attend an event, when he as the PM could never boast of mobilising 4000 from the entire populace, then he was certainly more influential.

The PM then asked for his secret and Munroe humbly replied that he had no secret but Jesus. The PM asked whether he could attend his next concert and Munroe boldly told him he couldn't. The PM was stunned and asked him why. To which Munroe replied that he would not want the concert to be misconstrued as a political rally. He eventually agreed to have the PM at the concert, when the statesman promised not to say anything at the event. Still, the PM was impressed with his comportment to the point of asking him the source of his wisdom.

When the concert eventually held with the PM in attendance, Munroe ministered and made an altar call, to which about 500 youth responded. Astonishingly, the PM too responded and gave his life to Christ. That became one of the major highpoints of life and ministry. He became a personal friend of the PM and his family from then till the former PM died in 2000.

At age 20 in 1974, Munroe was offered admission into Oral Roberts University, in Tulsa, Oklahoma, United States. He graduated in 1978 with a degree in Fine Arts, Education, and Theology. Two years later, he obtained a master's degree in Leadership, Administration and Business in from the University of Tulsa. He later received a doctoral degree in Philosophy.

Munroe returned to the Bahamas after completing his studies

in the United States and was soon employed in the Ministry of Education as Assistant Secretary to the Minister of Education. He also worked in the Department of Public Personnel under the Deputy Prime Minister.

BIRTH OF HIS MINISTRY

In 1980, while still working with the government, Dr Munroe started a Bible Study group in his apartment. There were six other people with him, making it a total of seven who were in attendance. The six were his wife (whom he had earlier married), his two brothers-in-law and their wives, as well as one of his friends from Oral Roberts University. The Bible study group soon grew into what has now become known as the Bahamas Faith Ministries International.

Dr Munroe's ministry received a major transforming boost when he went on a trip to attend a religious programme in Tulsa, Oklahoma. On one of the programme nights, the scheduled speaker, the late Archbishop Benson Idahosa of Nigeria, wasn't available. As if by divine arrangement, Dr Munroe was chosen to replace him. Fortunately, it was about the time he ministered that the media, including TBN and some radio stations, came around. And from that time on, his life story was rewritten and his international ministry was born. Book publishers, radio, and TV stations began approaching him, and being the purposeful person that he was, he leveraged on the open doors to fully unleash his ministerial vision.

Dr Munroe laboured assiduously, using revolutionary principles grounded in the scriptures to make a tremendous impact for the kingdom of God. As Bishop Paul Morton of the Full Gospel Baptist Church Fellowship International, said of him: "Dr Myles Munroe said "I will die empty." He would preach 2 hours while most do half that time. He did 80 years of preaching in 40 years of preaching."

Throughout his ministerial years, which spanned over three decades, he was known as a leader of leaders, best-selling author, multi-gifted teacher, internationally renowned life coach, versatile government consultant and leadership mentor to Fortune 500 Companies, and corporations.

He had over 50 books to his credit, many of which were bestsellers, distributing in more than 90 countries of the world. He also co-authored several other publications, as well as producing study guides and powerful audio and video tapes. He was a contributing writer for various Bible editions, journals, magazines, and newsletters, such as The Believer's Topical Bible, The African Cultural Heritage Topical Bible, Charisma Life Christian Magazine, and Ministries Today. He hosted a number of radio and television programmes, which were aired worldwide, reaching several millions of people.

Dr Munroe spoke and tutored extensively as a much sought after speaker, lecturer, educator and business counsellor. His ministerial success was seamless in scope and powerful in influence. Through his personal outreaches and various establishments he founded and headed, he ministered to individuals, churches, groups, governments, nations and continents. He was chief executive officer and chairman of the board of the International Third World Leaders Association and president of the International Leadership Training Institute.

With every opportunity, Dr Munroe made it obvious that his goal was to help people everywhere to discover their purpose and potential as God's agents of transformation on earth. His areas of focus covered Biblical exposition of Kingdom principles and critical issues that affect every aspect of human, professional, leadership, social, and spiritual development.

TESTIMONIES AND TRIBUTES

The most credible attestations of the awesome impact of Dr Munroe's ministerial influence actually come from the countless individuals, churches, organisations and nations he touched with his words and works. I will therefore devote the rest of this chapter to testimonies and condolences that poured in from religious ministers, celebrities and individuals from all around the world, as devastating reports of his home-going spread through social media.

William M. Wilson, President of Oral Roberts University (ORU):
His work in extending Christ's Kingdom in our generation was exemplary and world changing...His energy and enthusiasm for imparting Spirit Empowered Christianity to new generations was contagious. Whether in a leadership gathering with those in highest authority or in Bahamas as a caring shepherd in a community of believers, Myles was always the same -- upbeat, positive, loving, full of faith and searching for any way possible to make Jesus known in our generation. His loss will be felt around the world as well as in our hearts here at ORU.

Bishop TD Jakes, Senior Pastor of The Potter's House:
There are few biblical clinicians whose view of ministry wasn't enriched in some way by this tremendous bible scholar. His voice changed the way we viewed the Kingdom!

Ron Kenoly, worship leader and singer:
Myles and Ruth were close and dear friends to my family

and I. We worked together, we ministered together, and we stayed up many nights discussing Scripture, encouraging each other and celebrating the favour of our Heavenly Father upon our lives...Myles, you have always been a pillar of strength and a consistent encouragement to my family and I….Myles, I will always remember you for your charisma, eloquence of speech, long stories, wisdom and excellent delivery. You have set a very high standard for us to maintain.

Bishop David Oyedepo, President & Founder, LFCW a.k.a Winners' Chapel International:

A Poem

    Myles and I called ourselves 'twin brothers'
    Myles, my twin brother is gone up to glory
    Ruth, his partner in life and death has gone to eternal rest
    Faith and I miss you both! Our moments together on this side of the Jordan were most memorable.
    We stayed together on several occasions under the same roof
    We lodged in same hotels time and again; we shared the platform together preaching the good news of the Kingdom over the years.
    Our friendship of over 24 years was a most enriching and adventurous one,
    Our partnership in ministry was also a most profitable and rejuvenating one.
    Myles, my twin brother
    A bundle of inspiration
    A man of spiritual depth and insight
    A leader of leaders and teacher of teachers
    Ruth, a bundle of joy and divine radiance

Your smiles were ever contagious,
You exhumed gentleness, love and care like a fountain
You were indeed a priceless jewel!
The two of you were swifter than eagles
You literally traversed the globe
As you taught nations the principles of the Kingdom
You were both as strong as the unicorn,
Energetic, untiring, never relenting, purposeful and focused
I could still remember, Myles and I took all the inaugural induction lectures for the pioneer Faculty and Staff of Covenant University in August 2002.
All of Myles' meetings on our church platform were ever inspiring and impactful.
The Living Faith Church Worldwide really misses you!
Good night Myles, my twin brother!
Good night Ruth, his partner in life and in death

Bishop Neil C. Ellis, Presiding Prelate, Global United Fellowship:

One person can indeed make a powerful difference in the lives of many. One man, Dr. Munroe was a prolific, focused and effective Christian leader who served God selflessly and touched millions of lives. Dr. Munroe's teachings on leadership are profound and transformative.

As both of us hail from the same country and our ministries are less than a mile apart from one another, we shared a common brotherhood, with mutual interests and desires. I've always respected his passion for building real leadership. Dr. Munroe's ministry equipped leaders around the world to pursue excellence and to fulfil their grandest visions.

I encourage everyone to honor his memory by reflecting on

Dr. Munroe's essential words, "You weren't born just to live a life and to die, you were born to accomplish something specifically. Matter of fact, success is making it to the end of your purpose, that is success. Success is not just existing, success is making it to the end of why you were born. So, make yourself valuable by using your inherent gift to help humanity."

It has been my personal honor to know this great man of God, and again, we express our deepest condolences to the Munroe family, to the Bahamas Faith Ministries International Fellowship, and to the families of all who perished in this accident.

Paula White, Christian evangelist and TV personality:

My prayers & heart go out to the family & friends of Dr Myles & Ruth Munroe, BFMI. He touched my life & the world for God!

Deitrick Haddon, Gospel singer:

My heart is heavy and my eyes are filled with tears over the loss of such a powerful man of God. I read all of his books on the Kingdom and they opened my mind to the true concept of the kingdom."

Isabella Hurihe Hauses, CEO, Women of Substance Organisation (Namibia):

It feels like I lost someone personal. He was a father to me. He called me his daughter. He really poured himself out when he first came here (to Namibia) in 1996. Many of our leaders are following his leadership. He was somebody that meant so much. The world's not gonna be the same again. In as much as it hurts because of the way he died I will celebrate his life. I will pass on his principles and make sure he will not be forgotten. His principles will live forever, I have lost a father, I will carry the baton forward.

Ms Sarah Kagingo, Ugandan President's special assistant for communications:

He was very inspiring. He spoke to humanity no matter your faith. Even as a Muslim, I was touched and moved. He said the only thing worse than dying is living without purpose. His seven principles of the eagle also touched me.

Hamil R. Harris, Washington Post:

People anticipated something special every time Myles Munroe spoke. Whether it was a beautifully crafted sermon in front of thousands or the quiet advice he offered heads of state and corporate leaders, Munroe, a globally admired evangelist with ties to the Washington area, was known to offer a unique, simple wisdom.

Dr Eric Brown, President, Churches Together in England Pentecostal:

It was my distinct privilege to invite Dr Munroe as keynote speaker to several of our Pastors and Key Leaders' Conferences and on every occasion he spoke professionally and prophetically into the lives of our leaders. Indeed he was a frequent keynote speaker to many of the Evangelical, Pentecostal and Charismatic churches in this country. He was a gifted communicator, effective motivator, a man of faith and great courage and full of the Holy Spirit. He was a giant of our time and his unique place in the history of the Christian Church is secured.

HIS IMPACT IN DEATH

Bernice King, minister and youngest child of civil rights leader Martin Luther King Jr., made a powerful and thought-provoking statement about the passing of Dr Munroe, which has proved to be very true. She said, "whenever a Kingdom of God General like Myles Munroe is taken from us so abruptly, a cataclysmic shift is happening. Be still and know what God is saying to The True Church."

> **Indeed, Dr Munroe's impact did not end in his death. In fact his death actually confirmed the truth of the Scripture that when a grain of corn dies, it inevitably multiplies. His death has brought multiple blessings to God's Kingdom. So many people have been encouraged, inspired, revived and restored to the faith through this death. This confirms how God can turn negative situations into positive ones for His glory.**

Many people who had never heard Dr. Myles Munroe heard about his death, the words people were saying of him, and were moved to listen to him or read his books themselves. Many of these have wonderful testimonies to share and are actually wishing they had known him many years ago.

President of the School of Greatness Worldwide, Alex Ihama, wrote on hearing news of Dr. Munroe's transition, "Papa Myles, your passing has heightened our passion to build on your legacy of purpose, our quest to develop leadership in everyone all over the world, especially in the developing nations. Thank you for joyfully and completely pouring out yourself to the world. Rest assured that, like you, we shall rob the graveyard of our talents too, that we shall expend our potentials to enable millions of people to discover and fulfil their purpose in life. We are committed to living our lives to the fullest, like you did."

Also, co-founder of Heart and Hands Ministry, Nancy Elaine Minor, said it emphatically that the passing of Dr Munroe would indeed cost satan so many souls. She went on to pen down a prophetic poem she said God gave her on hearing about the news:

ARISE AND CROSSOVER!
Time for the church to ARISE
With fire in their eyes!
Time for souls to be won,
And God's Kingdom to come.
Established in hearts that are His own,
With self no longer on the Throne.
Time for this generation to come up higher-
Crying out "Come Lord Light Your Fire!"
Consume the sacrifice that is my life –
No longer betrothed but now a wife.
Glory and Grace and Grace and Glory!
Love's triumph is Calvary's story.
Victory won with the gate opened wide,
Whosoever will is welcome inside.
Go now and tell all that you meet-
And come and worship at His Feet.
Christ is seated on the Throne
HE bids you all welcome, so sinner come home

Another person shared this beautiful experience:
I was not a follower of Dr. Munroe, but after seeing the various posts on Facebook and video clips, I can only say I am totally touched by this great man's life. I have been so turned off for years with 'traditional' churches. The brazen presentation of money first and God second is disgusting. Yet, this man stood for the opposite--people first. I love his mantra 'make yourself jobless by imparting into others.' Wow, what a man!

Several other testimonies abound of the spectacular impact of Dr Munroe's death on people's lives and ministries throughout the world. Through this, we can begin to see other people who died young or in tragic circumstances in another perspective. Amazingly, most people had not heard of the other people who were on board the ill-fated aircraft until that incident. Ironically in their deaths, they have probably made more impact than the more than 7 billion people living in our world today.

Tell me which is better? They have made more positive impact for the kingdom of God in their death than when they were alive. They have made more news for the kingdom of God, in their death than maybe 99% of the people who are still living today because thanks to the news of their demise, a lot of people actually began to reconsider the essence of their lives.

More people than we can imagine are beginning to reconsider their purpose and putting their lives in order. Can you imagine how many people are rededicating their lives back to the Lord because of this situation? So many people are now getting to know the names of the victims of this crash and their families.

Again, I am not trying to say that the essence of our lives is to have fame, popularity in life or death but in this particular situation when Christians are being spoken about worldwide, as in the case of Dr. Munroe and his team, it has a ripple effect on the gospel. This means that people are one way or the other being touched to begin to think about the things of God, about their lives, about eternity, yet others are getting saved, becoming more dedicated to the Lord, renewing their faith and walk with God. Even such tragedy could bring more benefits to the Kingdom of God. Though it is at a very high price, when you think about the value of one saved soul in eternity, you can deduce that everyone who perished including Dr. Myles Monroe is presently rejoicing in heaven because their death has brought so much life to others.

Chapter 9

LIFE LESSONS FROM DR MYLES MUNROE

I mentioned in my introduction that my primary motive in writing this book is to make necessary clarifications and set records straight on the home-going of my friend and covenant brother, Dr Munroe, as well as to highlight its essence and the implications. I believe (and I do hope you agree with me) that this has been amply accomplished.

However, there is also a secondary motive – which is not too different from the motive behind most other biographies on extraordinary personalities. That motive is to highlight practical lessons from their journey to prominence, the salient character traits that made them successful, as well as the principles and philosophies that governed their lives and guided their destinies.

There are several lessons to imbibe from the life of Dr Munroe. From my personal interactions with him and from what others have been saying about him, I have extracted a few of these lessons in the following categories.

EMERGENCE FROM THE SHADOWS

Someone wrote, as a condolence to Dr Munroe:

"Here was a man who came to earth amidst challenges and turbulence. He made his way out of obscurity into limelight. Yea, more still bringing many out of their obscurity of darkness into divine security of greatness."

The writer was right. Who would have ever though that Myles, the sixth of eleven children born into a poor family and raised in a backwater community could end up as a global paragon of success, excellence and influence? Or to put it as a reporter once asked him, how did he transform from sleeping on a mat with rats to spreading the kingdom message around the world in a private jet?

The first thing I want to point out is that he was a man who never allowed the status of his family to determine the size of his dream. He dreamt big, despite growing up in a lowly environment. According to him, "People generally fall into one of three groups: the few who make things happen, the many who watch things happen, and the overwhelming majority who have no notion of what happens. Every person is either a creator of fact or a creature of circumstance. He either puts colour into his environment, or, like a chameleon, takes colour from his environment."

Rather than conforming to the limitations of his environment he chose to bring colour and honour to it. He had a firm belief in his dream and future. He upheld this same principle that he later taught millions around the world: "If you have hope for the future you have true riches; no matter how much you have in your account."

Secondly, he believed he was created to be an asset and not

a liability to the world. He believed God created him with a purpose and the greatest disservice he could do to himself and to the world was to expect something from the world, rather than purposefully seeking to influence the world with what God had deposited in him. In 2002, he shared some of this mentality with viewers of the Turning Point programme where he said, "My friend, listen to me - you were born to be a leader on earth representing God. You were born to make a difference and not just to make a living. You came to this earth, not just to pay bills but to pay your debt to society…God wants you to be an ambassador of the Kingdom of Heaven to bring his culture back to your city in every area of life."

Thirdly, he believed in creating opportunities out of adversities. This was a recurrent theme in his messages and he practised it consistently. He never complained about circumstances, he sought way out of them. His success story confirmed what George Bernard Shaw once said: "People are always blaming their circumstances for what they are. I don't believe in circumstances. The people who get on in this world are the people who get up and look for the circumstances they want, and if they can't find them, make them."

A good example of this was the instance I cited earlier when he launched a musical group but was not allowed in churches to sing. Rather than being daunted or embittered, he took the challenge to deliver his musical messages through another platform – concerts. That drive in him opened many doors of favours and opportunities.

I already mentioned how he became friends with the Bahamian Prime Minister through his concerts. That friendship, according to his own testimony, benefitted him in countless ways, granting him many privileges that otherwise might not have been there.

Fourthly, he was a good thinker who believed in using

personal initiatives to solve problems and make a difference. The constant desire to make a difference was one of the qualities that made him different from several other ministers of God. He was not one to conform to mediocrity in the name of maintaining the status quo. Whether in his approach to issues, managerial tactics or methods of delivering the Kingdom message, he was the quintessential strategist. That contributed to his success in many ways.

> **Rather than conforming to the limitations of his environment he chose to bring colour and honour to it. He had a firm belief in his dream and future. He upheld this same principle that he later taught millions around the world: "If you have hope for the future you have true riches; no matter how much you have in your account."**

I remember what happened when he was to start broadcasting Christian programmes in his native country, the Bahamas. There was a regulation in place that all religious programmes must be broadcast only on weekends. But he wasn't comfortable with that. He wanted his messages to be aired both on weekdays and weekends. When the regulators pointed his attention to the restrictive law in place, he gave them a reply, which left them with no choice but to grant his request. The reply had to do with what he had done earlier as a result of his foresightedness. He told them that he never registered his ministry as a church but as a non-profit organisation. Fortunately, the law was not applicable to such organisations and he was granted permission to broadcast on radio and TV any day of the week.

It was this same strategic thinking and passion to be different coupled with divine backing that made him successful in every other thing that he did. Consider his leadership influence also.

What made his so unique and impactful? He was dissatisfied with much of what he saw around in many so-called leaders in both the secular and religious spheres. "Leadership is birthed out of anger!" He said. "I was angry at things that are not the way they should be. In life, purpose is defined by the thing that makes you angry. Martin Luther was angry; Mandela was angry; Mahatma Gandhi was angry; Mother Teresa was angry. If you are not angry, you do not have a ministry yet."

Another quality that significantly helped him was his resolve to be a lifelong learner who believed in continuous learning development. He once said that "If you refine who you are, the Lord will expose you when you are ready." He thus never stopped learning and refining himself, even as he tutored and mentored others. And as he did, the Lord continued to "expose" him to greater opportunities for impact.

> **In addition, Dr Munroe was someone who recognised the power of productive synergy. Despite his numerous gifts, enormous influence and marvellous impact, he never for once imagined himself to be a super-minister who didn't need the support of other ministers or ministries. While he was aware of his strengths, he never failed to acknowledge areas where he needed to network with others in order to achieve maximum impact in life and ministry.**

Let me use his exact words:

> No one man can win the whole world but all men together under Christ can win the world. God will never place His programme in the hands of any one person or one ministry. He's too smart for that. But

He will make it necessary for all of us to have a piece of everything and that's why we need one another.

One of the weaknesses of the Church in history is the spirit of exclusivity and isolation. That's why denominations were developed. One move of God thought that it was the move of God and so they began to believe that previous or future moves could not be moves of God. This is very sad. The world seems to be wiser than us because it realises it has strength and it has weakness and that's why you have what they call merging companies. Some of the most successful companies in history are those that merged with other strong companies. The Church needs to learn that lesson and begin to network.

Networking is first understanding your strengths and weaknesses, appreciating the strengths of another and then joining your weakness to that person's strength so that you can be stronger. We will not make it in this 21st century without networking. Networking requires, first of all maturity, secondly, the ability to submit to another man's strength. Without those two added elements we remain prideful and weak.

However, the greatest of the propelling forces behind Dr Munroe's meteoric rise in ministry was his addiction to the Bible. It was one secret that he fortunately discovered so early in life and it worked wonders in his destiny and ministry. I already mentioned how he committed himself to reading the entire Bible every year from the age of 14. And as I pointed out, the impact of that decision was spectacularly far-reaching. The secrets he discovered in exploring the Scripture transformed his thinking; sharpened his reasoning about God, the world and his potentials;

brightened his vision of purposeful living; strengthened his resolve to be different; equipped him with principles and formulas for all-round success. He shared his testimony on this:

> I could say that I went from one state of life to another state of life by obeying, understanding, and applying these principles that are laid down in the Bible. I also discovered that the Bible is really not a religious book but a divine manual written by the manufacturer of humanity by which the product man is supposed to live. If we learn those principles and obey them, then we find that the process of failure to success becomes more inevitability than experiment.
>
> I can guarantee people, then, that if they learn, discover, understand, explore, and apply the same principles that I learned, that success is predictable. Failure or success is not race-related; it's not socioeconomics-related; it is really predictable, based on principles that are laid down by God the Creator by which we are supposed to function. If we find them and obey them, success becomes inevitable. That's why I was able to move from rats to 40,000 feet in the air in my own aircraft.

Still more interesting is that despite the avalanche of attention, admiration and accolades he received from all over the world in his lifetime, Dr Munroe remained so humble and unassuming. No wonder he continued to prosper in fulfilment of God's word that whosoever humbles himself will be exalted.

Everyone who encountered him had the same description of a man who saw them as equal and important to him, and thereby treated them with respect and warmth. More importantly, his humility was real and contagious. He related with people at all levels, across cultures and races, as if they were his siblings. Even in his outreaches, he was not discriminatory. As he ministered to big, wealthy congregations, so also did he to those smaller ones. Someone once shared a testimony of how he visited Zimbabwe in the mid '90's. He faithfully and gladly ministered there in a church that had no walls and the congregation was less than a hundred!

May Olusola of MannaEXPRESS magazine had this to say about Dr Munroe's humility: "I was privileged to interview Dr. Munroe on two occasions for MannaEXPRESS. His humility awed me. No ceremony, no bodyguards, no hordes of gatekeepers! Just a simple man with a burning Kingdom message for the world."

Someone from Nigeria also shared his experience after Dr Munroe's passing: "Dr Munroe visited my school while I was an undergraduate . . . Obafemi Awolowo University Ile Ife. I was shocked that such an International minister would accept to come and preach to us students. I was awed! That marked my mind."

In one of his interviews, Dr Munroe explained the reason behind his exceptional humility, despite being so blessed:

> "First of all, every human being was born with an inherent gift, and that gift is their gift to humanity; they are supposed to serve humanity in the area of their gifting…Your value in life is determined by the problems you solve through your gift. I encourage people to stay humble. One of the things that God told the prophet Elijah is, "Stay small in your own eyes." This is one of the greatest pieces of advice I ever heard. No matter how many people celebrate your gifts, don't ever think that you are more important to them than your gift is to them. This is why many people fail: They fail because they think that people

came to follow them. You must keep a careful, correct perspective on life that this is not about me but about me serving my gift to the world."

A REAL AND GENUINE LIFE

Dr Munroe's brand of Christianity was visibly authentic and practical. He believed in having a transparent life without hypocrisy or deceit, whether in public or in private. Actually, he had no reason to be superficial since he was not seeking the praise of men. As he once said, "Great leaders have no need for reputation. Reputation is what you are in public; character is who you are in private."

He preached what he practised and practised what he preached. He obviously agreed with the person who once said, "Live your life everyday with your biography in mind." Contrary to what often happens when some prominent ministers of God die and all sorts of scandals and cans of worms are opened about their private lives, Dr Munroe has departed now for about a year and all we have heard about him from those who knew him intimately as relatives, colleagues, members of staff and acquaintances, as well as those who knew him from a distance are testimonies of his impeccable character and exemplary lifestyle.

> **Dr Munroe's sincerity of life and purpose was evident in his fearlessness in declaring what he believed was the truth, regardless of where he was or who was involved. He never played to the gallery to please individuals, nor pandered to the whims of those in authority.**

I earlier mentioned how blunt he was in his teenage years towards the Prime Minister who had wanted to attend his gospel concert. That same candour continued to be reflected through his ministry. Even on issues that many ministers would have preferred to remain cowardly or compromisingly silent, he was vocal and unequivocal in his stance.

One of such issues was homosexuality. He was unambiguous in regarding it as unscriptural and unnatural. In 2014, following a gay pride event in his home country that seemed to attract the backing of some government officials, Dr Munroe released a statement to voice his concerns. Titled, *Homosexuality – Phobia or Principle?* It read in part:

> "In our postmodern world there is a massive deception invading the very moral fabric of nations and dismantling the very core of the natural existence of humanity. As matter of fact this deception is threatening the extinction of mankind. What is amazing is that this deception is not a new one, but it emerged in the context of human existence on the planet as long ago as five thousand years. However, despite the reality of its existence, it has historically always kept its place at the fringes of mainstream society.
>
> What is this deception? It is the unnatural attraction and relations between human species of the same sex or gender attempting to normalise the unnatural under the guise of being normal. Even though this unnatural behaviour disguises itself under many labels, it is generally described as Homosexuality. The word itself incorporates its basic premise and that is, it is primarily sex driven. Those who have decided to embrace, practice, encourage, and surrendered and succumb to its passions, and they desire to dignify, promote

and civilise this "lifestyle" over the past generation have become more aggressive even to the point of violence in some instances. This strategy seems to be one of fear mongering, psychological battery, and the selling of self-pity and abuse. Terms like bigot, hate crime, closed minded, conservative, anti-human, anti-civil, bullying, and the most common, phobia, are used to isolate the mainstream of humanity painting them as unloving, insensitive, ungodly, human haters, unsympathetic and uncivilised.

It is my view that this accusation of 'homo-phobia" is the greatest deception of all. Its intent is to make those who are considered 'normal' feel guilty for being normal. This deception is unfair, dishonest and dangerous. Its affect is to make the majority of humanity feel guilty for not accepting, glorifying and dignifying this 'unnatural' human behaviour."

Another aspect of Dr Munroe's commitment to living a genuine and practical life was his decision to remain focused on his particular calling. He loathed the idea of ministers of God dabbling into all sorts of practices and principles that are not in tandem with God's calling upon them. While he believed strongly in networking with other preachers, he wasn't one to be so mesmerised by what another person is doing to the point of sheepishly imitating and consequently veering off his own ministry. He maintained his originality, despite his congeniality. He kept to the same principle he recommended to others: "A true leader does not measure his success by comparing himself to others but by evaluating how he is fulfilling his own purpose and vision."

MARRIAGE AND FAMILY LIFE

Dr Munroe was a great husband to his wife, Ruth Ann, and a wonderful father to his two children. Despite his busy schedule, he was an amazing family man. He ensured that his wife and children were the primary beneficiary of his ministry of transforming people into leaders and leaders into change agents.

> **His love for his wife in particular was spectacular. They were together for 35 years, having been married since July 1979, and throughout those years, he never stopped cherishing, appreciating and celebrating her. In fact, it could even be said that so strong was their love for each other that death could not do them part – which was why they had to depart together.**

Dr Ruth had attended the same university (ORU) with her husband. However throughout their period of courtship, he never pressured her for sexual intimacy. Both decided to keep themselves pure before marriage. This was the same value he consistently taught youth and intending couples. He also often exhorted on the value of fidelity, using his own marriage as an example.

Dr Munroe practised what he taught and wrote about marriage. He personally believed and taught that one should not go out ministering to other people, if they had not ministered to their spouses. As an example of this, he once cancelled an early morning media appearance in his last visit to Kenya because he was going to have breakfast with his wife.

Indeed Dr Munroe was so devoted to his wife that all who knew them were fascinated and inspired by their daily exchanges of love. One day, one of their spiritual daughters, Ty Adams, asked

Lady Ruth what the most favourite thing to her in the world was. And she excitedly replied: "playing footie with your dad, it will never grow old."

The couple never argued, much less bicker. Ty narrated what Dr Munroe's once told her about this:

> My papa came home, just as we were sitting on the couch, and he came and closely nestled right behind her and embraced her, held her in his arms and said, 'Your mom is the essence of grace. Do you know we never argue, ever. Why? Because she is my beloved and given to me as a treasure from the Lord.'

Dr Munroe's love for his wife was not confined to their home. He demonstrated it as much as he had the opportunity even in public. Introducing her to a mammoth congregation during one of his programmes in 2004, he said: "I am very pleased to have with me the most beautiful, awesome, fantastic, exclusive, breath-taking woman in the world. Standing next to me is the essence of the quintessence of true love. I love this woman with all my heart, my liver, my lungs, my pancreas and everything within me. She is the answer to my prayer. This year we celebrate 25 years of marriage. I could not be what I am today without this wonderful woman. I want to stress seriously…to correct a historical mistake that I've heard people make again and again. That behind every good man is a good woman. I want to correct that. That should be "In front of every good man is a good woman…"

He ended the introduction by singing her a love song specially dedicated to her.

One of the people who knew the couple closely was Steve Strang of Charisma magazine. Here is what he said about Dr Munroe's marriage:

> He loved his wife, Ruth, and theirs was an example

of what a healthy Christian marriage should look like. One of the first times I heard him speak, he called her to the podium and told the audience how beautiful, smart and beloved she was, using flowery poetic language that made me wish I could be that romantic in such an elegant way. I learned that saying the right thing at the right time inspires other husbands in a positive way to do the same. Of course my wife is very private, so I'd never invite her to the podium. But, I think Myles' example made me more conscious of how to be more expressive in how I articulate my deep devotion as a husband. Myles and Ruth seemed to have a wonderful marriage during the three decades I knew them.

Perhaps, the most instructive aspect of his love for her was allowing her grow and develop in her calling as a wife, mother and co-pastor in the church. Unlike many men and so-called ministers of God, he never felt intimidated by his wife's vision or vibrancy. Rather than relegate her, he elevated her in such a way that her significance and role in his life and ministry could not be disputed. Apart from being a Senior Pastor of their church, Bahamas Faith Ministries International (BFMI), she was also Vice Chairman of the Munroe Group of Companies in Nassau, Bahamas.

Beyond that, he gave her maximum opportunity and support to develop her potential. No wonder she travelled around the world with him, equally teaching the message of the kingdom and training leaders for maximum impact. She founded and presided over the Women of Excellence Ministry at Bahamas Faith Ministries International. She also consistently ministered to pastors' wives around the world, encouraging them to discover their individual purpose. She was named among the leading women of the Bahamas for her participation in the growth of women in leadership.

Having carefully taught millions and patiently mentored thousands around the world, it is no surprise that Dr Munroe's daughter, Charisa Makaria, and son, Myles Chairo Jr. have grown to be as "plants grown up in their youth" and "pillars, sculptured in palace style" (Psalms 144:12). Nurtured with sound scriptural principles in a loving home by godly parents, the two children have become beacons of excellence in their own rights.

They are living examples of the manifold blessings that accrue from parents investing quality time in training, guiding, helping, teaching and mentoring their children to become champions in life. Today, both children are playing colossal roles in preserving, upholding and projecting the legacies of their father.

Speaking of his children at one time, Dr Munroe proudly said: "My son, 29 years old, is running my businesses. My daughter, who is 30, is running our global organisation. Why? I mentored them."

A TEACHER WITH DISTINCTION

This was one area in which Dr Munroe decidedly distinguished himself as a minister of God. He was a teacher with distinction, precision and unforgettable impartation. From the beginning of his ministry, he determined to spend more time on teaching than preaching, citing Jesus Christ as his example. When asked why he preferred to teach than preach, he replied:

> In my humble view, the difference between preaching and teaching is very important. To preach means to declare, to pronounce or to announce. To teach

means to train and instruct for change. Preaching doesn't change people. Preaching may attract, give information, alert people, even convict people, but teaching brings understanding and you cannot change until you understand. You cannot grow until you have information. That's why Jesus taught. Jesus never preached to the disciples. He preached to the multitudes, but He taught His disciples. He announced the Kingdom to the multitudes but He taught the Kingdom to His disciples.

What was the focus of Dr Munroe's teachings? Kingdom principles. He taught the application of the principles revealed in the scriptures in every area of life – spiritual, marital, career, financial etc. I think this is because those same principles had greatly transformed his life and he wished others would discover the manifold secrets that he and many other had discovered. He once explained the reason behind his focus on the principles of God's Kingdom:

> The reason why principles are so important is because principles make life predictable. In other words, God designed life in such a way that it is very simplified. Principles are laws that are established by the creator or the manufacturer by which a product functions. If you violate those laws, then you produce malfunction, which is what we call failure. If you obey those laws and align yourself with those laws, then you are guaranteed success… My greatest fear is that the spirit of religion is lurking in so many churches today. Instead of men and women of God preaching about and applying Kingdom principles to everyday living, they have

given the spirit of religion the power to cloud the path of others. I admonish everyone reading this article to read Matthew, Mark, and John and reconnect with the Kingdom. If we place our trust back in the source, which is God Himself, He has principles laid out by which He wants to take care of you. Even though you are in the world, you should not be of the world system.

The manner in which Dr Munroe delivered his teaching and the impacts on people's lives truly confirmed that he was meant to be a teacher. His revelations about principles of the Kingdom were insightful and illuminating. What's more, unlike most preachers and teachers of the word, his goal was not to teach to keep the people in the nest, his goal was to inspire them to get out of the nest to fly and become who God had created them to be. It is no wonder he was sought after globally and his books stood out as best-sellers, with millions of copies sold worldwide.

His knowledge, interpretation and application of scriptural principles have enlightened, empowered, emancipated and equipped millions around the world to discover their destinies and align with them. Many solid relationships have been built and many marriages have been repaired and restored through the outstanding wisdom revealed in his teachings.

Someone who read one of his books testified that, "about ten years ago, I bought a book titled Rediscovering the Kingdom. I was just about to graduate from high school and attend college. After reading the book, I was so enlightened through revelation of the kingdom that by the time my freshman year began I believed I could literally conquer anything, and that my heavenly Father owned everything. I felt so empowered. So strong. I walked with such confidence and authority. I was so excited about what I had learned, I began sharing the message of the kingdom with my colleagues, and with great enthusiasm. I will be forever grateful for the wisdom of Dr. Myles Munroe."

A LOVING PERSONAL TOUCH

In a 2012 *Turning Point episode*, Dr Munroe said, "I never desired to be a minister. I desired to help people".

That was indeed true of his passion as a minister and mentor. He showed genuine interest in people and went to great lengths to meet their needs and alleviate their pains. I myself have been a beneficiary of this on several occasions, one of which I mentioned in the Preface.

Many others have testified to this personal touch which they consider so amazing and inspiring for a man of his calibre. Bishop Vernon G. Lambe Sr., Senior Pastor and General Overseer of the First Churches of God, Bermuda, once shared his experience with him. He said after he had published his first book, he was so nervous of how it would be received or criticised. He took a chance and sent a copy to the great men he knew around the world, including Dr Myles.

Interestingly, while most of the people never replied, to the bishop's very shock, Dr Myles, in the midst of one of his extremely busy schedule, wrote him a letter of encouragement signed by himself. The bishop was really startled because he knew how busy Dr Munroe's schedule was. He was so touched that he kept the letter for a memorial.

Dr Munroe indeed proved what he taught: "The greatness of a man is measured by the way he treats the little man. Compassion for the weak is a sign of greatness."

A GLOBAL MENTOR

In fulfilment of his mandate of raising change agents, Dr Munroe successfully raised millions of top class world leaders after his kind. Many of these he directly mentored through his leadership mentoring programme. However the bulk of his mentees were the hundreds of thousands he did not know personally because they were scattered all around the world. As most of these would later testify, even though he did not know them individually, they were over the years building their lives, homes and ministries according to the teachings and principles he taught through his publications and sermons.

Here, I will share the experiences of two of his mentees.

The first of these is **Coach Felicia,** a Certified Empowerment Coach, author and trainer, who won the 2012 "North America's Next Greatest Speaker" honour. Here is her narration, as published in Essence magazine:

> It was nearly 25 years ago, I heard him speak for the first time. A failing college student in the throes of depression, I clung to his teachings on purpose with a quiet desperation. Every day, I lived with a seemingly bottomless emptiness. I longed to hit rock bottom because at least I would know things couldn't get worse. I would meet him in person four years later. Tagging along with my sister and future brother in-law, I found myself at a dinner table with this powerful visionary. Still insecure and struggling, I listened while everyone around me talked.
>
> It was suddenly quiet and I then realized that he was talking directly to me. He asked me to share one of

my poems. I nervously conceded and when I finished, he looked in my eyes and told me my future—that my words would travel the world and change lives.

Dinner continued, but from that moment on my life changed. He dared to speak what I had longed for in my heart—for my life to have meaning. To others at that table I may have been no one worth noting, but he saw my potential! And he dared me to release it.

I met his beautiful wife Ruth a few years later. She was a woman who stood in her own strength and purpose. Knowing her identity enabled her to embrace others with a warmth and kindness few can parallel. She understood that it was her relationship to him that empowered him to be who he was to millions.

I am confident that time and history will reveal the true magnitude of the impact the Munroes had on the world and generations to come.

Today, I can say that you are reading this column, because 20 years ago as I hid from my own shadow—my mentor challenged me to live! He told me I was born to make a difference and I believed him—even when I did not believe in myself.

I know that the best way to honor their legacy is to live the messages they literally gave their lives to share.

We don't get to determine our life's entrance or exit, but we do get to decide its impact and content. Today, I encourage you to live fully and stop fearing the power of your gifts.

Death is certain, but living must be a decision. Give all that you can to this world and be determined to die empty!

Another of his mentees is life coach and inspirational speaker, **Trista Sue Kragh**. She narrated (to the Beliefnet magazine) five lessons she gleaned from his example that everyone can all learn from.

Tell your story

Papa Myles was really adamant about me telling my story. He would say 'people need to know your story'. So now that's what I'm doing, working on a book entitled, "Figure It Out." Most of it is my story and it's really interesting because I'm utilizing the principles I learned from both my biological father and my spiritual father and then taking those principles and tying them back into the Word of God. It's a book that empowers others to become who they were called to be and make the changes necessary to fulfil their purpose.

Speak the original truth to others

All he did was tell us the original truth about who we are and who God is. The Kingdom message resonates with your spirit when you hear it because it reminds us that we were born for something bigger than ourselves. So my goal is to encourage others to cancel all excuses and get them to believe that they can do what they were born to do.

Don't toil in life

"When you latch on to what God says about you and reject the naysayers, you don't toil in life. You become so focused on your purpose and passion it protects you from needlessly expending energy in areas outside of God's will. It really upsets me when I see people in this state because if they only knew the truth they would be set free."

Leadership is self-discovery

When you become yourself, automatically you become a leader. We all have the potential, but you can't just decide to be a leader...you have to become you or better yet God's original idea of you. Sadly, most people die as followers because they never discover who they are, their purpose or potential. Leadership in its simplicity is the self-discovery process.

Generational problem solving

Your purpose will solve a problem that your generation needs, but first you have to take the steps of: becoming yourself, discovering your purpose, identity, who you are and writing out your life vision. This is the formula for success and once you do this...then you become influential and start getting people's attention.

> In fulfilment of his mandate of raising change agents, Dr Munroe successfully raised millions of top class world leaders after his kind. Many of these he directly mentored through his leadership mentoring programme. However the bulk of his mentees were the hundreds of thousands he did not know personally because they were scattered all around the world.

Chapter 10

THE LEGACIES OF DR MUNROE'S LIFE

I f there is anything people all around the world, who had the privilege of relating with or listening to Dr Myles Munroe could testify about his life, it would be that he was a man of purpose who passionately believed that one's life must be lived for something that will outlast it. He consistently maintained throughout his eventful earthly sojourn that "the value of life is not in its duration, but in its donation."

It is for this purpose that I will be briefly looking at some of the donations that Dr Munroe made to the world before his home-going. Certainly, as testimonies and reports have repeatedly shown, his influence and impact on people's lives globally can never be quantified or imagined. What I wish to do however is to highlight some of the visible endowments he bestowed on the world that are meant to perpetually bless the human race even long after his departure.

These endowments or legacies include:
- His church.
- His leadership organisations.
- His impact on The Bahamas and the third world nations.

HIS CHURCH – THE BAHAMAS FAITH MINISTRIES INTERNATIONAL (BFMI)

I already mentioned how the foundation of the BFMI was laid in 1980 as a Bible Study group consisting of Dr Myles and Ruth Munroe and five others. Dr Munroe had, despite having a lucrative government job decided to obey the divine mandate to start the group. Amazingly, that little seed that was sown in 1980, soon grew into a full-fledged worship center, now known as the Bahamas Faith Ministries International (BFMI).

Through Dr Munroe's unwavering passion for the manifestation and expansion of God's Kingdom, as well as his Spirit-controlled leadership capabilities, The BFMI was developed into a massive edifice of God's Kingdom, under which shade various categories of people of all races, ages, cultures, backgrounds, social circles and educational attainments – gather to receive divine revelations and inspirations leading to a productive and prosperous life.

People from all parts of the world throng the headquarters of the BFMI in Nassau, the Bahamas, as they saw it as a fountain ever overflowing with revelations of the bountiful riches of the Kingdom of God. Others simply go there, like the biblical Queen Sheba, to ascertain the secrets behind the success story of the BFMI, which stands out as a multi-faceted international centre of revolutionary teaching, training, equipping and empowering of individuals to discover, develop, deploy and maximise the potential of their inherent gifts and purpose.

What is most interesting about it all is that Dr Munroe ensured that the BFMI does not just serve as a church or denomination, but as a Christian growth and resource centre. With a vision slogan that says, *"Transforming Followers Into Leaders And Leaders Into Agents Of Change,"* the BFMI functions as a network of ministries and agencies that provide for the development, training and release of purpose-driven, spiritually sound, character-based, and confident individuals motivated by their conscious responsibility to maximise their inherent leadership potential.

As a pragmatic and visionary leader who taught many governments and corporations around the world on effective leadership, one would naturally not expect anything less from Dr Munroe on his own primary project, the BFMI. Every aspect of the ministry's operations reflects the purposefulness and discipline of the founder. To actualise and sustain the ministry's objectives, special attention were given to its various departments, which include: the Real Men Ministry, the Women of Excellence Ministry, the Youth Alive Ministry, the Children's Ministry, the Singles Ministry, the Marriage Ministry, the Fine Arts Worship ministry, the Media ministry, the Evangelism & Missions ministry, and the Diplomat Publishing ministry, among several others.

Through these departments, Dr Munroe and His beloved wife, together with a host of men and women whom they had mentored, ensured the evolution of the BFMI into a community with a lifestyle reflecting Heaven's culture, a community where everyone from every part of the world wants to join and no one wants to quit. This was made possible, not just through Dr Munroe's illuminating teaching and training sessions but also his conscious development of practical programmes for discovering, understanding and applying the precepts, keys, principles, values, morals, and standards of the Kingdom of Heaven on earth.

> Someone once said that Dr Munroe, in his death, passed on so many batons, which would make his passing a multiple-fold blessing and not a loss. I believe the departed Kingdom luminary did this primarily through the vibrant and purpose-driven men, women, youth, children who he raised through the various departments of the BFMI.

The most glaring evidence of the legacy that Dr Munroe left through his church is contained in a statement released after his home-going, part of which reads:

> Dr. Munroe taught us to have faith and to pursue purpose and advance the Kingdom Principles of Jesus Christ here on earth. He also taught us to be leaders. As a Church body and organization we will move forward as Dr. Munroe would have wanted us to. We recognize that there will be challenges but we have full confidence that God will see us through and we intend to make our founding leaders proud.

As a demonstration of Dr Munroe's powerful legacy through the BFMI, the ministry has continued to carry on with his Kingdom ministrations as if nothing drastic had taken place. This affirmed what Dr Munroe himself once said that he had mentored and developed so many people who could effectively continue the great work he had started should he be absent for any reason. In fact, shortly after his passing, a message was posted on the Facebook page of the BFMI that the Global Leadership Forum he was on his way to attend before the crash happened would go on as scheduled. The message was appended with this inspiring note: "This is what Dr. Munroe would have wanted"!

This year alone, in furtherance of Dr Munroe's Kingdom vision, the BFMI, through its new Senior Pastor, Dr Dave Burrows, has been engaged in numerous activities, projects and programmes aimed at advancing God's Kingdom. With the year's vision, Kingdom Impact and Influence, the ministry continues to get stronger, equipping and training every member for deployment into the world.

HIS LEADERSHIP ORGANISATIONS

One of the greatest consolations from Dr Munroe passing is the fact that he had replicated himself in hundreds of thousands of leaders in the world. This he achieved through:

- **The International Third World Leaders Association (ITWLA)** - which he birthed with the goal of addressing the critical need for quality, effective leadership development and training, especially in emerging developing nations, as well as offering assistance to Third World countries.
- **The International Third World Leadership Development Foundation** – which he established with the goal of providing an opportunity for individuals, organizations and corporations to invest in the various leadership programmes of ITWLA. His ultimate goal in establishing the foundation was to ensure that capital development projects in Third World and Developing Countries are supported and assisted by resources from the Foundation, as well as providing Leadership Assistance and Training to these countries.
- **The International Leadership Training Institute (ILTI)** – which Dr Munroe founded with the goal of

meeting the needs of leaders at all academic levels beyond high school who desire to become international, inter-cultural, inter-disciplined statesmen and women in every discipline.

Through their various programmes, projects and outreaches, these organisations continue to function effectively in nurturing creative and transformative leadership in Third World countries all over the world.

HIS CONTRIBUTIONS TO THE BAHAMAS

The truth of the saying that charity begins at home was never lost on Dr. Munroe. While reaching out to peoples, nations and governments around the globe, he ensured that his country, the Bahamas received a larger share of his attention and influence. He was a consummate nationalist with unmistakable desire for the spiritual, economic and social advancement of his nation. From the time he completed his education in the United States in the late 1970s he was deeply involved in making meaningful contributions to the affairs of his country directly and indirectly.

Dr Munroe contributed directly in building his nation by:
- Taking up government jobs, where he distinguished himself meritoriously before going into ministry full time.
- Acting as a consultant and counsellor to successive governments throughout his lifetime.
- Engaging in advocacy and constructive criticisms. A good example of this was the case I cited on the gay parade event which had the support of certain people in government and which Dr Munroe openly and unequivocally denounced.

THE LEGACIES OF DR. MUNROE'S LIFE

He contributed indirectly by:
- Boosting the tourism industry through the huge number of people from all over the world who thronged the Bahamas to attend his programmes or see him personally.
- By influencing and mentoring great leaders, entrepreneurs and statesmen holding key positions in government and making remarkable impact on the progress of the Bahamian nation.
- Providing employment opportunities for hundreds of staff who worked in his establishments.

> **He was a consummate nationalist with unmistakable desire for the spiritual, economic and social advancement of his nation. From the time he completed his education in the United States in the late 1970s he was deeply involved in making meaningful contributions to the affairs of his country directly and indirectly.**

Let me summarise the contributions of Dr Munroe to the Bahamas with the words of the current number one man in the nation itself – the Prime Minister:

> "I don't have to tell you that Dr Munroe really loved his country, this beloved Commonwealth of The Bahamas. Yes, he would go forth into the world, crisscrossing continents, flying across the great oceans of the planet but he would always come back home to play his part, a leading part, in helping to build up his country.
> This kind of outreach was central to his sense of purpose and central to his work as an evangelist for Christ because it was clear to me that religion for Myles Munroe was not about locking oneself up in some

remote ivory tower of private contemplation. Rather, it was about rolling up your sleeves and getting down into the trenches to deal with the real problems of real people living in the real world.

So let us make no mistake about it therefore : while Dr. Myles Munroe was unquestionably a globalist, an internationalist, in the scope of his Christian ministry and in the reach of his teachings and travels, he was, at the same time, a profoundly committed nationalist; a Bain Town-bred Bahamian through and through; a man who never forgot his roots; a man who was passionately involved in Bahamian nation-building and who played an important part in that process over the course of more than three decades."

The greatest testimonies to his colossal contributions to the Bahamian nation lie in the numerous ways in which he was recognised and honoured. Dr. Munroe was the country's youngest recipient of the 'Queen's Birthday Honours' Order of The British Empire (OBE) Award 1998 bestowed by Her Majesty, Queen Elizabeth II, for his spiritual and social contributions to the national development of The Bahamas. He was also honoured by the government of The Commonwealth of The Bahamas with the Silver Jubilee Award (SJA) for providing twenty-five years of outstanding service to The Bahamas in the category of spiritual, social and religious development. Following his death, he was given a state-recognised burial with key dignitaries in government, including Her Excellency Dame Marguerite Pindling, Governor General; The Rt. Hon. Perry Christie, Prime Minister; Leader of the Opposition Dr. Hubert Minnis; Senators, Members of Parliament, Senior Government Officials, members of the Diplomatic Corps and leaders of the international religious community.

Chapter 11

DR. MUNROE'S REVELATIONS TO THE WORLD

One of the monumental legacies that Dr Myles Munroe bequeathed to the world is the wealth of timeless and priceless revelations about the Kingdom of God. He was evidently a seasoned life-coach with an uncommon anointing to unearth, explain and apply life-changing principles from the Scriptures to every aspect of life. His insights were always deep and his perspectives were always unconventional – which always had people astonished and awakened.

As I have previously noted, Dr Munroe's sphere of influence as a leader, teacher, mentor and consultant was both diverse and dynamic. He seemed to be ever overflowing with inexhaustible ideas and strategies for all-round success for all individuals, families, organisations, governments and nations around the globe. This informs why he seemed to be constantly on the go, as he was regularly bombarded with invitations from all quarters and corners of the earth to impart words of life and wisdom to them. And as the dutiful minister and ambassador of Christ that he was, he did his best to honour the invitations, using every opportunity to point attention to godly solutions to the numerous questions and challenges of humanity.

Dr Munroe's treasuries of Kingdom principles are contained in his vast teachings, many of which, thanks to technology are preserved in his numerous writings, publications, audio tapes and DVDs; and, above all, the countless lives and homes which were transformed and continue to be inspired by his impartations.

I will be presenting here some instructive and inspirational insights from Dr Munroe's teachings on selected topics that have been of immense benefits to me as an individual. These include:

- His kingdom message
- His message of purpose
- His leadership message.
- His message of hope to the third world
- His message of turning followers to leaders.
- His celebration of family values.

MUNROE ON GOD'S KINGDOM

Dr Munroe's exposition of God's Kingdom is not only enlightening but also emancipating and empowering. Actually, the number one focus of his ministry was teaching the message of the Kingdom and unlocking its secrets and principles. He once declared that, "a true minister of God that really wants to represent Jesus should preach nothing else but the Kingdom…I find it hard to imagine that there can be another message from me beyond the Kingdom message. For me, the Kingdom message is unsearchable, it has no end; unfathomable! The Kingdom is inexhaustible."

With this uncommon vision and drive, he taught, challenged, and inspired millions around the world on the Kingdom message. He transformed many from being mere churchgoers to Kingdom believers, as he revealed mysteries of the word of God to them. Through his Kingdom message, many who had become bored and disillusioned by monotonous church attendance and rituals discovered that there was more to Christianity than they had been exposed to. It was as if scales were removed from their eyes as they saw for the first time the boundless riches, privileges and authorities they had as citizens of the Kingdom. His teachings on the Kingdom God completely changed the way they saw themselves, the world and even the word of God. Their minds were transformed and their relationship with God changed for the better entirely.

Even those who thought they knew about the scope and purpose of the Kingdom were amazed as Dr Munroe expounded the Scriptures, revealing more uplifting aspects of the Kingdom and taking people's understanding to a whole new, empowering level. He was so passionate about emphasising the Kingdom perspective as the only way to help believers truly understand who they are, as well as their rights and privileges as children of God.

Dr Munroe revealed that this passion of his actually stemmed from the fact that the whole Bible, along with the message of Jesus, revolved around the Kingdom and not a religion. He emphasised that this is the same message that Christ wants every Christian and every denomination to focus on. According to him, "we are here, sent from our heavenly home to colonise earth with the Kingdom of heaven…You came to this earth, not just to pay bills but to pay your debt to society and to give them the good news that they can come back to God's country on earth…God wants you to be an ambassador of the Kingdom of Heaven to bring his culture back to your city in every area of life."

Dr Munroe also noted that one of the reasons Christians must take the gospel of the Kingdom seriously is that we cannot fully enjoy the boundless benefits of God's Kingdom until we understand how it operates. He believed there is so much transforming impact the message of the Kingdom will have on our lives and destinies. Most of the problems and deficiencies in churches today result from ignorance about the Kingdom.

Dr Munroe particularly expressed concern over the church's focus on mere religion rather than focusing on practical applications of Kingdom principles. He emphasised that merely focusing on religious thinking and practices leads to bondage instead of liberation. On the other hand, once a person understands Kingdom principles and learns to apply them to his or her life, life takes on new meaning and empowers such a person to live a fruitful and victorious life.

Dr Munroe made a rather striking point between religion and the Kingdom saying, "Jesus Christ did not bring a religion into the world. He bought a Kingdom. The world doesn't need another religion. It doesn't need traditions and rituals. The world needs a practical application of principles and precepts that will impact their daily lives. Jesus said blessed are those who are poor spiritually for to them belong, not a religion, but the Kingdom of heaven. Only the Kingdom satisfies spiritual hunger – not religion."

Especially on the personal and ministerial levels, Dr Munroe taught that with the right perception and application of the concept of the Kingdom, every believer automatically possesses the keys to unlock success in every area. However, contrary to what some think, Dr Munroe's Kingdom messages were not just focused on prospering on earth; he also frequently reminded believers that as true citizens of God's Kingdom on earth, they are merely temporarily passing through a foreign land before getting to their home in heaven.

As I already mentioned, Dr Munroe's Kingdom revelations and expositions were overwhelming impactful throughout the world. Many have testified that just listening to him for the first time changed their perception of Christianity and transformed their lives and ministry for good. One minister of God wrote of the impact of Dr. Munroe's Kingdom teaching on her ministry:

"Dr. Munroe was profoundly instrumental in the pivotal shift in our ministry. Until 2007, we had been a church, however God instructed us to learn about His Kingdom and led us to read Dr. Munroe's books and watch his video teachings to deepen our understanding. We became a Kingdom Training Centre shortly thereafter. God was shifting us out of Tradition into Kingdom. I can never express my gratitude for all that Dr. Munroe taught us. His legacy will live on in those of us that he mentored through his books and teachings based on his revelation of God's Kingdom. He was faithful to his earthly kingdom assignment, and I am grateful for all that he had to endure to walk in obedience to God to release that revelation. His legacy shall continue to live on in the lives of those that he has mentored through His books and videos. I am eternally grateful for them and determined now more than ever to fulfil my purpose and advance God's Kingdom in the earth."

MUNROE ON LEADERSHIP

Leadership was a key part of Dr Munroe's Kingdom message. It was what he spent the greater part of his ministry teaching and demonstrating. In fact, as at the time of his home-going, he was on his way to his annual leadership programme, where many had gathered to listen to his often unconventional and thought-provoking insights on the subject of leadership.

Dr Munroe's devotion to the subject of leadership is grounded in his belief that leadership is the number one purpose of God for creating mankind. He once declared that, "the original purpose for mankind, defined and established by the Creator, was to "rule (have dominion) over all the earth." Since the word "dominion" in this case means to reign and rule, the Creator wired all humans with the capacity and natural ability to lead. We can conclude that human beings are wired for leadership."

Dr Munroe believed and taught that "Trapped within every follower is a hidden leader." Thus, his life's focus was to help as many people as possible, of every nation, race, creed, or social status, to discover their true leadership potential. He defined leadership as "the capacity to influence others through inspiration motivated by passion, generated by vision, produced by a conviction, ignited by a purpose."

He emphasised however that becoming a true leader begins with a solid relationship with God who equips us to discover our leadership capacities and fulfil them. He said, "True leadership is not something you obtain by doing steps 1,2,3, but by connecting to your source, your designer, your creator, and allowing this power to flow through you will empower the Spirit of Leadership to surface and be revealed."

Dr Munroe equally distinguished between leadership spirit and the spirit of leadership. He noted that while leadership spirit is the inherent leadership capacity and potential that is the essential nature of human beings; the spirit of leadership is the mind-set or attitudes that accompany a true leadership spirit and allow the dormant leadership potential to be fully manifested and maximized.

He emphasised clearly that understanding this difference is

critical for discovering and living out one's leadership capacity. What he meant by this is that it is one thing to know that one was born to lead, but it is another thing entirely to cultivate the habits, attitudes and competencies needed to be an effective leader.

Dr Munroe also noted that true leadership is not one implemented through force or arrogance, but one that thrives on willing submission and humble service to others. He said, "there are many people, past and present, who have influenced others using threats and violence, but we don't call that true leadership. We call it manipulation, oppression, or dictatorship. Nero, Hitler, and Idi Amin were all influential. They exerted their wills over people, but they were not leaders in the true sense."

> **Leadership was a key part of Dr Munroe's Kingdom message. It was what he spent the greater part of his ministry teaching and demonstrating. In fact, as at the time of his home-going, he was on his way to his annual leadership programme, where many had gathered to listen to his often unconventional and thought-provoking insights on the subject of leadership.**

One essential lesson that Dr Munroe taught on leadership is that leadership is not just about charisma but about CHARACTER. A leader must be a man of sound character, as character flaws can destroy his leadership capacity and ministry. On the importance of character to leadership, he emphasised the following:

- The foundation of leadership is character.
- No matter what type of leader you are or how widespread your influence, you face personal temptations, challenges, and stresses. And only a foundation of character will sustain you and your leadership.

- Character is when people around you can predict what you are doing when no one is watching.
- Character means one doesn't have a secret life. It means a person is the same in the day and the same in the night.
- Character is self-imposed discipline.
- Character is a commitment to set of values without compromise.
- Without character, a leader will crumble sooner or later.

MUNROE ON TURNING FOLLOWERS INTO LEADERS

Dr Munroe clearly stated that, "the passion of my life is to help as many people as possible, of every nation, race, creed, or social status, to discover their true leadership potential." He believed that true leadership fundamentally requires the responsibility of taking followers into the exciting unknown and creating a new reality for them.

But not only did he believe and lived out this passion, he actually taught it severally to other leaders, urging them to make raising up leaders a key focus of their lives and ministries. According to him, the greatest act of leadership is mentoring. Thus, to test the real measure of a leader's impact or success, one should observe what happens in his or her absence. He said, "If all you have done dies with you, you are a failure."

Dr Munroe taught that a leader's legacy should not be in buildings, programmes, projects or other lifeless things; he emphasised instead that a true leader's legacy is his investment in people – identifying, training, guiding and developing people who can take after him and replace him if need be. He once said: "True leaders make themselves unnecessary. A true leader works themselves out of a job."

Dr Munroe believed that Jesus Christ is the epitome of this leadership strategy, which he encourages everyone to imbibe. He taught that Jesus clearly told his disciples that it was better for Him to go away so that their potentials and greatness could manifest fully. And as proof of that, the ministry of Christ grew mightily after His departure. The secret was His painstaking mentoring of His disciples over the years to continue after Him.

Every leader who wants to be seen as being successful must equally imbibe this example from Jesus Christ. In reference to his own principle and practice on this leadership style, Dr Munroe has a challenge for every leader today:

> "My question is, if you die today…what happens to your organization, what happens to your church, what happens to your business? If it dies when you die, you are a failure.
> So I encourage you right now, identify your successors, and mentor them, and train them. This is why in our organization, I am unnecessary. I can travel the world and our ministry grows."

MUNROE ON PURPOSE

Dr Munroe taught that, "The greatest tragedy in life is not death, but a life without purpose." His teachings on purpose, through his books and sermons, were practical, incisive and life-changing. He helped millions through his teachings to discover their purpose, unlock their potentials and do great and mighty things for God and society.

Dr Munroe defined purpose as "original intent" or "reason for creation." He emphasized that every single individual on earth has a purpose, which God created him or her to fulfil.

Beyond that, however, every individual equally has the capacity to fulfil his purpose because his peculiar features and characteristics have been designed by God to aid the fulfilment. He emphasised his reason for firmly believing in this principle by citing the example of manufacturers, who usually have detailed plans and purposes for their products before embarking on manufacturing and marketing. He taught that God is even more purposeful and strategic in his creative works; so no one should see himself or herself as worthless or talentless in life.

> **Dr Munroe clearly stated that, "the passion of my life is to help as many people as possible, of every nation, race, creed, or social status, to discover their true leadership potential." He believed that true leadership fundamentally requires the responsibility of taking followers into the exciting unknown and creating a new reality for them.**

Dr Munroe emphasised the need for every individual to ascertain, develop and stick to their purpose in life. He once gave an illustration about a pastor who was given a ministry to serve a group of nine people. Dismissing the original mission, that pastor became a huge worldwide success with a large congregation. When he died and came face-to-face with God, he started to talk about all of his achievements and work for God while on earth. God listened to all he had to say and when he had finished, God said "well, that's good for you, but what about the nine?" By this, Dr Munroe taught that we all shall give account to God on what we achieved with our purposes. God would seek to know how many lives we impacted and how much contribution we made to His Kingdom through our purposes.

Still on the indispensability of establishing the essence of one's existence, Dr Munroe maintained that except this is done, an individual would end up abusing his or her destiny and jeopardizing God's programme for his or her life. He taught that, "where purpose is not known, abuse is inevitable."

Most importantly, Dr Munroe emphasised that discovering, upholding and fulfilling God's purpose is the key to ultimate fulfilment in life. "You can never be totally and completely satisfied until you find your purpose and then live in it. You cannot do what you are supposed to do until you discover what you are supposed to do. And doing what you are not supposed to do will not bring fulfillment into your life. You are wasting time. You are abusing your life. And that must stop!"

MUNROE ON THIRD WORLD NATIONS

As a minister of God, Dr Munroe's passion for third world nations was unparalleled. In fact, he seemed more concerned about such nations more than their own clergymen. Even though these nations are currently battling several challenges, Dr Munroe remained ever optimistic about the programme of God for them. Here is his message of hope for the third world nations:

> I am convinced that the last world on earth is the third world; that God has now turned His face toward them. I am convinced that the greatest spiritual movement on earth is about to emerge and it will not emerge from the first world or the second world. It will emerge from the third world. It has already begun. I am a part of it. I represent them. The largest churches that exist today and the massive growing emerging ministries are in developing countries.
>
> I believe that God is going to transfer the responsibilities

for winning the world in this century to the third world people. Also keep in mind that the largest segment of the world's population is in third world countries. So it is very natural for the Lord by His wisdom to move among those people to win their own people. If the second and first worlds are wise, they will begin to learn from the third world and find out what's going on and not to try to impose their brand of Christianity on the third world because it will not and cannot work. God is raising up people without anyone's permission. He is calling them. He is anointing them without anyone's sanction and the greatest leaders in the world to come will be third world leaders used of God. They are going to be products of their culture and God is going to use them to impact the world. And my prayer is that the second, first and third world believers will cooperate and not compete with each other and see the world won for Jesus.

For this hope to be realised, Dr Munroe further offered practical suggestions for holistic transformation in the third world nations. He said in one interview concerning people of the third world:

The only ones that can reach these people are the people themselves. I believe that the greatest way to win the third world is to win the third world people first and let them go back into their own culture and into their own environment and share the Gospel. One of the greatest obstacles is the misconception of who Jesus is. Many third world people I work with have a concept of Christ that comes from what religion calls Christianity. In many ways Christianity has misrepresented Christ in a very terrible way. I'm talking about hundreds of years of history that has really damaged the image of Jesus. Many of these people don't want to hear about Christianity.

Secondly, in many of these countries there are very strong cultic religions, and those religions have also twisted the concept that people have of Christ. We need to correct that. Thirdly, in many of those countries there is a misconception of God and the reason why Christ came to earth. We have misrepresented and almost made Jesus Christ synonymous with democracy. That's dangerous because Christ is a King, not a president.

Finally, poverty and corruption are major issues in many of these countries because of poor leadership that was a product of oppression. People have been dispossessed. They have been raped of their dignity, their self-concept, self-worth and self-respect. Christianity is not enough as a religion. These people need restoration of self-concept and in many cases the religion of Christianity does not provide these answers. Many times it can provide the religion but it doesn't provide restoration of the quality of life that people need to have to believe in themselves. So these are some of the issues that we need to look at in the 21st century and I hope the Church will take another look at what makes effective missions.

To the men in third world nations in particular, Dr Munroe gave a message of hope, reassurance and inspiration:

"Remember, your past is not your future, and you are not a victim of your history. I challenge you to embrace the joy, responsibility, and honor of being a male made in the image of God. You have an obligation to restore the true image of manhood and to establish a model for our sons of this new generation. It is now your time to be proud to be a Third-World man. The first-world man of Europe has failed to present the picture of the true man of God's image. The second-world man of the New World and industrial revolution has also failed to present the original image of God's man. Now you are the last world, the final world, the Third World. It is your turn to rediscover the original meaning of what it is to be a real man and to represent the image of God to a world that is in desperate need of a male prototype who will also restore purpose to the female and to children. It is your turn. Do it for our children, and make a difference."

MUNROE ON MARRIAGE

Dr Munroe's teachings and revelations on marriage are revolutionary in building and keeping a successful home. His insights are enriching and all-encompassing, covering every aspect of relationship and family life. Dr Munroe taught that marriage should not be taken lightly and that divorce should never be an option - according to God's plan.

He taught on the weightiness of marital vows and why they must be kept:
A promise is a commitment to do something later, and a vow is a binding commitment to begin doing something now and to

continue to do it for the duration of the vow. Some vows, or contracts, are for life; others are for limited periods of time… Marriage is two imperfect people committing themselves to a perfect institution, by making perfect vows from imperfect lips before a perfect God

He taught on the supremacy of God's word in guiding couples conduct in marriage:

Every conscientious husband and wife should measure their marriage by the unchanging standard of the principles found in God's Word… We will never obtain God's kind of marriage simply by going along with the crowd, doing what everybody else does. We have to dig deep into the heart of God to discover His principles.

He taught on practical love in marriage:

Love in marriage is more than just a feeling or an emotion; it is a choice. Love is a decision you make anew every day with regard to your spouse. Whenever you rise up in the morning or lie down at night or go through the affairs of the day, you are choosing continually to love that man or that woman you married.

Love is an ongoing debt that we owe each other, a debt that should never be paid off. Paul made this clear when he wrote to the believers in Rome, "Let no debt remain outstanding, except the continuing debt to love one another, for he who loves his fellowman has fulfilled the law" (Rom. 13:8). If we get into the habit of thinking of ourselves as always owing a debt of love to our spouses, we will be less inclined to take offense when they say or do something that we do not like.

The people most successful at both giving and receiving love are not the ones who walk around degrading and bad-mouthing themselves all the time, but those who are fully in love with themselves and fully aware that they are loved by God. Because they are at peace within themselves about themselves, they are free both to give love and to allow others to love them.

He taught about fidelity in marriage and further expanded its meaning:
Marital faithfulness involves more than just sexual fidelity. Being faithful to your wife also means defending her and affirming her beauty, intelligence, and integrity at all times, particularly before other people. Faithfulness to your husband means sticking up for him, always building him up and never tearing him down. Marital fidelity means that your spouse's health, happiness, security, and welfare take a higher place in your life than anything else except your own relationship with the Lord.

He taught on the role of husbands:
Headship is not rulership; it is leadership. As head, the man is to provide spiritual leadership and direction to the family. He is supposed to chart the course. His spiritual temperature should set the climate for his entire house…God did not create woman from man's head, that he should command her, nor from his feet, that she should be his slave, but rather from his side, that she should be near his heart…Within the overall context of loving his wife, a husband's first and primary role is to be the spiritual head and covering and teacher in the home. Through his words, lifestyle, and personal behavior the husband should teach the Word, the will, and the ways of the Lord to his wife and children.

He taught on the scope and benefits of submission in marriage:
Submission means that a wife acknowledges her husband's headship as spiritual leader and guide for the family. It has nothing

whatsoever to do with her denying or suppressing her will, her spirit, her intellect, her gifts, or her personality. To submit means to recognize, affirm, and support her husband's God-given responsibility of overall family leadership. Biblical submission of a wife to her husband is a submission of position, not personhood. It is the free and willing subordination of an equal to an equal for the sake of order, stability, and obedience to God's design. As a man, a husband will fulfil his destiny and his manhood as he exercises his headship in prayerful and humble submission to Christ and gives himself in sacrificial love to his wife. As a woman, a wife will realize her womanhood as she submits to her husband in honor of the Lord, receiving his love and accepting his leadership. When a proper relationship of mutual submission is present and active, a wife will be released and empowered to become the woman God always intended her to be.

He taught about judicious management of finances and resources:

If we hope to become effective and successful in life, ministry, and especially marriage, we have to learn to be good managers. Stewardship means being accountable to God for every resource under our care. Effective managers do more than simply keep things running; they add value to everything they have responsibility over. Under a good manager, resources will appreciate in value... All married couples should examine themselves periodically and ask, "What have we done with the resources God has given us? How are we handling His blessings? Are we spending our money wisely? Have we progressed over the past year? Are we moving in the direction God wants us to go? Are we obeying His will? Is He pleased with our management? What does He want us to do next?" These are important questions for growing in stewardship.

Basic stewardship of resources for married couples who are believers centers around understanding and practicing two fundamental financial principles: tithing and budgeting. Herein lie the seeds of dominion—the secrets of fruitfulness, increase, and filling. Tithing recognizes God as the source of our resources while budgeting recognizes our responsibility"

He taught about honest and meaningful communication between couples

Communication is the ability to ensure that people understand not only what you say but also what you mean. It is also the ability to listen to and understand others. Developing both of these aspects of communication takes a lot of time, patience, and hard work...When trying to communicate with each other, a husband and wife should be careful to make sure their voices and faces agree with their words.

He taught about selflessness in marriage:

Satisfied needs produce fulfilled people, and fulfilled people are free to pursue and exercise their full potential as human beings. The primary goal, then, in any relationship should be the meeting of needs. We should not concentrate so much on meeting our own needs, but those of the other person in the relationship. A good test for the health of a relationship is to ask ourselves periodically whose needs we are meeting, ours or theirs? If we are focusing on our needs, the relationship is in trouble. In successful, healthy relationships, both parties put a priority on meeting the needs of the other.

He taught about limits of parental interference in marriage:

Once a man and woman have married, the only thing they

should receive from their parents is advice and counsel, and then only when they ask for it. Parents should not offer opinions or advice without being asked. To do so undermines the development of the leadership and self-determination of the couple. When they married, the leadership and decision-making responsibilities transferred from their former homes to the new home they are building together. All leadership now devolves on them. They are responsible for making their own decisions. Part of cultivating companionship is learning how to exercise these responsibilities effectively together.

He taught on understanding the differences between the genders, with the aim of helping couples understand each other better:
1. Men and women have perfectly complementary designs.
2. When men and women don't appreciate their differences, they experience conflict. When they value each other's purposes, they can have rewarding relationships and blend their unique designs harmoniously for God's glory.
3. Until the male recognizes the strengths God has placed within the female, he will be weak in those areas, because she is designed to supply what he lacks.
4. The primary needs of males are (1) respect, (2) recreational companionship, and (3) sex. The primary needs of females are (1) love, (2) conversation, and (3) affection.
5. A male is naturally a —logical thinker, while a female is naturally an —emotional feeler.
6. A male generally expresses what he's thinking. A female usually expresses what she's feeling. To a male, listening to spoken language is a process by which he receives information. For the female, it's an emotional experience.
7. Men are often like filing cabinets: they make quick decisions

and mentally file them away, or they create mental —to do folders, filing away problems until a later time. Women are generally like computers: their minds keep working through problems until they are solved.
8. In material things, men usually want to know the details of how to get there, while women tend to look at the goal. In spiritual things, the opposite is often true.
9. A man's job is an extension of his personality, while a woman's home is an extension of hers. A man's personality is fairly consistent, while a woman's is continually changing.
10. Men are nomadic, while women need security and roots.
11. When encountering something new, men tend to stand back and evaluate. Women are more ready to accept new experiences, and they participate in them more easily.

MUNROE ON FAMILY VALUES

Dr Munroe taught extensively on developing and upholding strong family values. As with all his other messages, his teachings on family values are profoundly practical and inspiring. Personally, as a man and a father I have learnt many unforgettable lessons from him on how to be a good father. Let me share some of what he said here: "He helped me when dealing with relationships and how I need to be whole as a single first."

1. A Good Father Knows the Heavenly Father

A man won't be able to understand what it means to be a good father if he doesn't know His heavenly Father. When Jesus rose from the dead, He made this wonderful statement: "I am returning to my Father and your Father, to my God and your God" (John 20:17). Because of Jesus' death and resurrection on our behalf, we can know God not only as our Creator but also as our Father.

A man must also have faith in God as His Father—that He will love, protect, and provide for him. Trust and reliance on God is what a father needs to model for his children. The greatest heritage a man can leave his sons and daughters is not money or property, but faith. A house can burn down, or someone can sell or repossess it, but no one can destroy the faith you have instilled in your child. Besides, the child will be able to use his faith to obtain another house, because he has been taught to trust God as his Provider

2. A Good Father Loves the Mother of His Children

The second most important thing a man can do for his children is to love their mother. Many men buy gifts for their children, such as bicycles and computers, when what the children want and need most is to see their fathers truly love their mothers. I think there is nothing more precious than for a child to see his parents being affectionate with one another. I think kids get a feeling of security when they see that. Showing consideration and respect for your wife is extremely important. Are you demanding and impatient with your spouse, or do you treat her with kindness and understanding? What are you modeling for your children about what it means to be a husband? Children take in everything they see, and your children observe the way you treat your wife much more than you may know. A child will often lose respect for his father if he doesn't see him giving his mother the consideration and love she deserves.

3. A Good Father Loves His Children

Many parents think love means providing their children with clothes, food, and shelter. That's merely a natural and moral duty. Anyone with common sense and a little bit of conscience would buy food. Love is much more than that. There are fathers who pay the rent for their children, but don't go to visit them. There are fathers who buy their children Christmas gifts, but send them with somebody else. Buying things for your kids doesn't necessarily mean you love them. It may mean you feel guilty about not fulfilling your responsibility to them. Some men don't even want to do that. They don't pay child support, so the courts have to deal with them. Love is not buying gifts. Love is you being a gift. The Bible tells us that our heavenly Father so loved the world that He became a revelation of that love in Jesus Christ. Therefore, if a man is really a father, he doesn't just send gifts. He sends himself. That's the essence of love.

4. A Good Father Is Responsible for His Children.

There is a popular idea today that every person should take total responsibility for himself or herself, no matter how young that person is—that a child has —children's rights that are the same as an adult's. This philosophy teaches that a parent cannot spank a child as a disciplinary measure. If this happens, the child should be able to go to court and get an injunction against his parent for hurting him. It also says a child should also be able to —divorce his parents. What the world is saying is that children should be allowed to bring themselves up. This idea is foolish. You don't treat children as adults. Children are children; grown-ups are grown-ups. Sometimes adults act like children. But children are definitely not adults and shouldn't be treated as if they were. Parents have a responsibility before God to raise their children. God does not leave the care and upbringing of your children to themselves or to society. He leaves it to you. How much time do you spend with your children? Who is really bringing them up? Perhaps you and your wife leave for work early in the morning and don't return until late in the evening. You don't see much of your children. Someone else has brought them up all day. Realize that everything that person represents goes into your children. They will learn their views of God, their concept of themselves, and their philosophy of life from their caretaker. You need to be careful whom you allow to watch your children.

5. A Good Father Teaches and Instructs His Children

A father needs to read and study the Word of God so he can teach it to his children. He must know the commands of God. It's impossible to teach something you haven't learned yourself. Remember what God said about Abraham, whom He called His friend?

> "Abraham will surely become a great and powerful nation, and all nations on earth will be blessed through him. For I have chosen him, so that he will direct his children and his household after him to keep the way of the LORD by doing what is right and just."
> **(Gen. 18:18–19)**

God made a promise to Abraham and said the fulfillment of the promise was connected to Abraham's teaching his family the Word of God. There's a relationship between the two. God is holding up some fathers' blessings because they aren't loving their children enough to teach them the Word

6. A Good Father Trains and Disciplines His Children

In Hosea 11:3–4, God said,

> "It was I who taught Ephraim to walk, taking them by the arms; but they did not realize it was I who healed

them. I led them with cords of human kindness, with ties of love; I lifted the yoke from their neck and bent down to feed them."

"It was I who taught Ephraim to walk." God was talking about His people. He was saying, —I have always been with you. From the time you were a child, I was working with you. When you fell down, I picked you up. I was training you. That's the spirit of a father. Our heavenly Father takes a personal interest in our training. Likewise, we are to personally train our children. Proverbs 19:18 says, "Discipline your son, for in that there is hope; do not be a willing party to his death." This is serious business. The verse is saying, —Discipline and train a child now because there is hope in that discipline, hope in that training. You are giving hope to your child when you discipline and correct him. You are giving him a value system for his entire life. The Scripture says if you don't do this, you're a party to your child's death.

7. A Good Father Encourages His Children
First Thessalonians 2:11–12 says,

> "For you know that we dealt with each of you as a father deals with his own children, encouraging, comforting and urging [or warning] you to live lives worthy of God, who calls you into his kingdom and glory."

This passage gives us three additional responsibilities of a good father: encouraging, comforting, and warning. First, children need encouragement. Some children never hear an encouraging word from their fathers. Do you hear how some fathers talk to their children? They act as if the children can't do anything right. A ten-year-old boy is washing the dishes. His father comes in and says, —Can't you clean dishes better than this? The little guy is at least trying. So encourage him. Maybe he leaves a little soap on the stove or counter. Don't look at what he left; look at what he cleaned up. Encourage him.

8. A Good Father Comforts His Children

Next, children need comforting. You encourage them when they're doing something positive, and when you want them to improve in something. But there will be times when they become discouraged, hurt, confused, or disillusioned. That is when they need comfort. How can you comfort your children? By letting them know they are loved, even when they make mistakes or don't live up to your expectations. By listening to their struggles and problems with kindness and understanding. By giving them warm embraces and loving words when they are sad. To be a comforter, you have to be accessible to your children. You have to know what's going on in their lives so you can know when they're going through struggles and loneliness.

9. A Good Father Warns His Children.

Fathers are also to urge or warn their children to live righteously. Yet how many fathers confuse warning with threatening? —I'm going to kill you if you don't stop that! Some fathers don't have any kind of tact, because they don't know any better. A child interprets a warning as love, but sees a threat as hate.

10. A Good Father Does Not Provoke His Children

Last, fathers need to be careful not to provoke their children. The Bible says, "Fathers, do not exasperate your children" (Eph. 6:4), or "Do not provoke your children to anger" (NASB). What are fathers to do instead? "Bring them up in the training and instruction of the Lord" (v. 4). Fathers have a way of provoking their children by impatience or harshness. Yet sometimes provocation means more than we normally think of in connection with the word. Notice that the above verse refers to "training" and "instruction" as the opposites of provocation: —Don't provoke, but train. Don't provoke, but instruct. Provocation can mean neglect. When you neglect your children, you incite them to despise you. Some fathers have no sensitivity to their children's needs, so the children become exasperated, provoked. They end up with inferiority complexes and undeveloped personalities, because their fathers didn't show them the love and kindness of God.

LAST WORD

Indeed, time and space will not permit me to reveal all I wish to say about this exceptional and remarkable hero of faith. However, the overriding message in every chapter of this book is clear and credible: Dr Myles Munroe's home-going was not a calamity – it was a divinely calculated arrangement to usher him to his well-deserved rest and reward, and to cause a cataclysmic revolution in the Church through an explosion of the Kingdom principles throughout the world.

Rather than question God or lament, we should appreciate God for what He did through Dr Munroe's life, as well as celebrate and uphold the legacies of the man who rose from the ghetto to become a LEGEND.

Above all, we must reflect on our lives and the legacies we wish to leave after we're gone. Are you living your life with purpose and with the understanding that your time may be up any moment? What will you be remembered for after you're gone?

Let me leave you with the words of this song by C.T Studd:

"Two little lines I heard one day,
Traveling along life's busy way;
Bringing conviction to my heart,
And from my mind would not depart;
Only one life, 'twill soon be past,
Only what's done for Christ will last.

Only one life, yes only one,
Soon will its fleeting hours be done;
Then, in 'that day' my Lord to meet,
And stand before His Judgement seat;
Only one life,'twill soon be past,
Only what's done for Christ will last.

Only one life, the still small voice,
Gently pleads for a better choice
Bidding me selfish aims to leave,
And to God's holy will to cleave;
Only one life, 'twill soon be past,
Only what's done for Christ will last.

Only one life, a few brief years,
Each with its burdens, hopes, and fears;
Each with its clays I must fulfil,
living for self or in His will;
Only one life, 'twill soon be past,
Only what's done for Christ will last.

When this bright world would tempt me sore,
When Satan would a victory score;
When self would seek to have its way,
Then help me Lord with joy to say;

Only one life, 'twill soon be past,
Only what's done for Christ will last.

Give me Father, a purpose deep,
In joy or sorrow Thy word to keep;
Faithful and true what e'er the strife,
Pleasing Thee in my daily life;
Only one life, 'twill soon be past,
Only what's done for Christ will last.

Oh let my love with fervor burn,
And from the world now let me turn;
Living for Thee, and Thee alone,
Bringing Thee pleasure on Thy throne;
Only one life, "twill soon be past,
Only what's done for Christ will last.

Only one life, yes only one,
Now let me say, "Thy will be done";
And when at last I'll hear the call,
I know I'll say "twas worth it all";
Only one life,'twill soon be past,
Only what's done for Christ will last."

FOLLOW PASTOR SUNDAY ON SOCIAL MEDIA

Subscribe And Read Pastor Sunday's Blog:
WWW.SUNDAYADELAJABLOG.COM

Follow These Links And Listen To Over 200 Of Pastor Sunday`S Messages Free Of Charge:
WWW.GODEMBASSY.COM/MEDIA

Follow Pastor Sunday On Twitter, 5 Words Of Wisdom Daily:
WWW.TWITTER.COM/SUNDAYADELAJA
…And Suggest Your Friends To Follow As Well!

Join Pastor Sunday's Facebook Page To Stay In Touch:
WWW.FACEBOOK.COM/PASTOR.SUNDAY.ADELAJA
…And Suggest Your Friends To Join As Well!

VISIT OUR WEBSITES FOR MORE INFORMATION ABOUT PASTOR SUNDAY'S MINISTRY:
http://www.godembassy.com
http://www.pastorsunday.com
http://www.churchshift.org
http://sundayadelaja.de
http://sundayadelaja.com
http://www.adelaja.com

About Pastor
SUNDAY ADELAJA

Sunday Adelaja is the founder and senior pastor of the Embassy of God in Kiev Ukraine and the author of more than 300 books which are translated in several languages including Chinese, German, French, Arabic, etc.

A fatherless child from a 40 hut village in Nigeria, Sunday was recruited by communist Russia to ignite a revolution, instead he was saved just before leaving for the USSR where he secretly trained himself in the Bible while earning a Master's degree in journalism. By age thirty-three he had built the largest church in Europe.

Today, his church in Kiev has planted over a thousand daughter churches in over fifty countries of the world. Right now they plant four new churches every week. He is known to be the only person in the world pastoring a cross cultural church where 99% of his twenty five thousand members are white Caucasians.

His work has been widely reported by world media outlets like Washington Post, The wall street Journal, Forbes, New York times, Associated Press, Reuters, CNN, BBC, German, Dutch, French National television, etc.

Pastor Sunday had the opportunity to speak on a number of occasions in the United Nations. In 2007 he had the rare privilege of opening the United States Senate with prayers. He has spoken in the Israeli Knesset and the Japanese parliament along with several other countries. Pastor Sunday is known as an expert in national transformation through biblical principles and values.

Pastor Sunday is happily married to his "princess' Pastor Bose Adelaja. They are blessed with three children, Perez, Zoe and Pearl.

BOOKS BY PASTOR SUNDAY ADELAJA

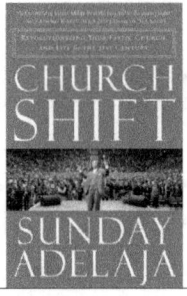

Churchshift: *Revolutionlize you faith, Church and life for the 21st Century.*

Money Won't Make you Rich: *God's Principles for True Wealth, Prosperity and Success.*

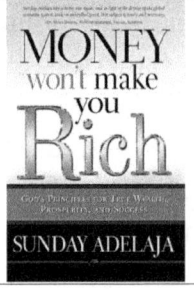

Time is Life: *History Makers Honor Time.*

Pastoring Without Tears: *It is possible to live and minister without sorrow and grief.*

Olorunwa (There is God): *Portrait of Sunday Adelaja. THE ROADS OF LIFE.*

CONTACT

For distribution or to order bulk copies of this book, please contact us:

USA
CORNERSTONE PUBLISHING
info@thecornerstonepublishers.com
+1 (516) 547-4999 . www.thecornerstonepublishers.com

AFRICA
Sunday Adelaja Media Ltd.
Email: btawolana@hotmail.com
+2348187518530, +2348097721451, +2348034093699.

LONDON, UK
Pastor Abraham Great
abrahamagreat@gmail.com
+447711399828, +44-1908538141

KIEV, UKRAINE
pa@godembassy.org
Mobile: +380674401958

www.ingramcontent.com/pod-product-compliance
Lightning Source LLC
LaVergne TN
LVHW051831080426
835512LV00018B/2822